Wooden Banks You Can Make

by Harvey E. Helm

Fox
Chapel Publishing Co. Inc.

1970 Broad Street • East Petersburg, PA 17520 • www.foxchapelpublishing.com

© 2002 Fox Chapel Publishing Co., Inc.

Wooden Banks You Can Make is a brand new work, first published in 2002 by Fox Chapel Publishing Company, Inc. The patterns contained herein are copyrighted by the author. Artists purchasing this book have permission to make up to 200 cutouts of each individual pattern. Persons or companies wishing to make more than 200 cutouts must notify the author in writing for permission. The patterns themselves, however, are not to be duplicated for resale or distribution under any circumstances.

Publisher	Alan Giagnocavo
Editor	Ayleen Stellhorn
Desktop Specialist	Linda L. Eberly, Eberly Designs Inc.
Cover Design and Photography	Keren Holl

ISBN 1–56523–173–2

To order your copy of this book,
please remit the cover price
plus $3 shipping to:
Fox Chapel Publishing Company
Book Orders
1970 Broad Street
East Petersburg, PA 17520

Or visit us on the web at
www.foxchapelpublishing.com

Printed in China
10 9 8 7 6 5 4 3 2 1

Because working with a scroll saw inherently includes the risk of injury and damage, this book carries no guarantee that creating the projects described herein is safe for everyone. For this reason, this book is sold without warranties or guarantees of any kind, express or implied, and the publisher and author disclaim any liability for any injuries, losses or damages caused in any way by the content of this book or the reader's use of the tools needed to complete the projects presented herein. The publisher and the author urge all scrollers to thoroughly review each project and to understand the use of any tools involved before beginning any project.

<u>Acknowledgments</u>

To Joan, my wife of 40 years. Without her love, encouragement and patience, this book
would not have been possible.

To Pam, my daughter, who typed the text for me to edit.

To Ayleen, my editor, for her patience, encouragement and help.

Thank you!

Table of Contents

Cat Bank, page 14

Panda Bank, page 38

Flower Bank, page 22

Turtle Bank, page 52

About the Author

Harvey E. Helm

Harvey E. Helm has been working with wood since he was about five years old. His father would stand Harvey on a wood packing crate so that he could cut shapes on his father's 24-inch scroll saw. The task not only kept young Harvey busy, it also instilled in him a great love for woodworking.

Woodworking has followed Harvey throughout his entire life. He received a teaching degree and taught high school industrial arts. Many of the bank patterns in this book were developed as projects for his students. The Piggy Bank on page 40 was the first bank that Harvey designed specifically for his students.

Currently retired, Harvey lives in Florida with his wife of 40 years. He enjoys making scrolled gifts for his family, especially his 10 grandchildren. In addition to substitute teaching in the local high school's industrial arts program, he is also an advisor on woodworking for the Florida chapter of the Blind American's Association.

Getting Started

Welcome to the banking business—wooden, that is. The banks in this book were developed over many years. They are the results of my students wanting to make something other than foot stools or bookshelves during our industrial arts classes.

The first bank we made was the piggy bank in 1976. From then on, the students would say, "You ought to make a whale bank;" and in a day or two, we would be making whales. Some of the designs came easily. The owl, for example, was designed and built on one of my lunch breaks. Others, like the rooster, took more than a year to develop. The point is, you can design your own bank using the same general ideas in this book. Ideas for designs can come from any source: newspapers, magazines, hobbies, professions... anything!

These banks are very simple to make, but please read the directions first. Also, just because a group of industrial arts students can make them, do not think they are only for kids. I am sure that some will be a challenge, even for those of you who are experts.

Tools

The construction of these banks is very simple, and few tools are required. I would advise you to buy the very best tools you can afford, as they will give you longer use, generally will work better, and will be more economical in the long run. With few exceptions, it does not pay to buy cheap, throwaway tools.

All of the banks in this book can be made with hand tools. Power tools will make much of the work easier. I recommend the starred items (*) as "nice to have."

To get into the bank business you will need the following tools.

• *One scroll saw* and a package of the necessary blades.* Either a scroll saw, a band saw or a coping saw will work well for cutting these patterns. Avoid scroll saws that use springs to tension the blade. Most parallel arm saws will do a good job. Look for a smooth cutting action, an easy blade changing mechanism, and a throat capacity that will handle the work you intend to do. Keep extra blades handy. You will break a few before you are done. I use mostly #2 blades to get a smooth, fast cut.

• *One drill.* I recommend a low cost ⅜-inch capacity electric drill. Eggbeater-type drills are often available at yard sales or flea markets. Battery drills are the modern version. This should be at least a 12-volt drill; the lower voltage drills are often lacking in power.

• *Drill press.** This will help you make straight holes with less effort. Check the horse power, chuck capacity (½ inch is good), length of quill travel and distance from chuck to comb.

• *One hole-saw set.* The nesting kind with seven sizes from ¾ inch to 2½ inch is fine, but a mandrel and individual saws are of much better quality.

• *Assorted twist drill and spade bits.* These can be purchased as needed.

• *Files and rasps.* A one-half round cabinet file 8 inches long, plus a good file handle. You will also need a one-half round cabinet rasp. Note: The file handle is very important. A poor one will hurt your hand and fall off and be a real annoyance. Try the handle first to see if it is comfortable.

• *Sanding sticks.* Great sanding aids can be made from small wooden sticks, like tongue depressors. Simply cut the sticks to the size and shape that you need; then glue sandpaper to the sides. Spray

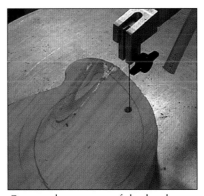

Cut out the centers of the bank parts on a scroll saw. A starter hole drilled in the cut-out portion of a bank's center piece gets you going.

adhesive will hold the sandpaper in place, but carpenter's glue is better.

• *Disc sander.** These machines save a lot of work in smoothing the wood. They come in 6-inch, 8-inch, 10-inch and 12-inch diameters.

• *Small router.** This tool is very handy for rounding edges. I recommend at least a 1HP model. Try making your own table for your router. There are many plans available.

• *Vise.* You will need a means of holding your work secure. If you have a workbench with a vise, great! If not, a small vise clamped to a table will do.

• *Clamps.* If you are going to make your banks without using nails, you will also need some clamps for holding the pieces together until the glue dries. These can be wide-opening spring clamps (4¼-inch wide) or wooden hand screws (more expensive, but better). The new one-hand clamps work very well for gluing these projects.

• *One claw hammer.* Choose a 13 oz.

• *One accurate ruler, tape measure or folding ruler.* Do not use a school ruler or a yardstick as these are not accurate.

Materials and Supplies

• *Wood.* All the banks in this book can be made from 1-inch by 8-inch lumber and ½-inch by 8-inch lumber. (Note: A 1-inch by 8-inch board will actually measure ¾-inch thick by 7½-inch wide; and a ½-inch by 8-inch board will be ½-inch thick by 7½-inch wide.) I use pine mostly, as it is the least expensive, easiest to cut and most available in my area; but any wood will do. Some of the banks—the moose bank on page 75, for example—are made from a combination of

Everyday household items make circles that are just as perfect as those from a template.

different woods. Other banks use ⅛-inch Masonite or plywood.

Visit a local cabinet shop or other woodworking business and inquire about their scrap or waste. If you stay out of their way and do not bother them, they will usually be glad to have you haul away scrap. The biggest piece of wood you need for these banks is ¾-inch by 5 ½-inch by 8 ½-inch. In some cases, you can use plywood. The stripes from the plies look very decorative, but be sure there are no voids (holes) in between the plies that could show up on the edge of the bank. This would spoil the appearance of the finished bank.

• *Glue.* Any good glue for wood is okay, but yellow (aliphatic) glue is the best. It has more grab and sets faster than white (casein) glue, which is a big advantage. Many times you can glue the parts together without clamping and resume working in as little as one hour's time.

Try this little experiment: Take two small pieces of wood, spread yellow glue on the surface of one (a thin coat will do), and place the second piece onto the glue. Slide them back and forth a few times to spread the glue. Set the pieces aside for five to ten minutes. You will have considerable difficulty getting them apart, if you can at all. Try the same test with white glue and you will see the advantage of yellow glue. Yellow glue can also be sanded, which is very important in this work.

• *Template-making equipment.* You will need some paper, light cardboard, and a Number 2 pencil. Pencil marks are easier to remove from wood than ballpoint pen or other ink marks. Kindergarten pencils—the fat ones—are great for marking wood. They give you a very dark line that is easy to remove or erase.

• *Sandpaper.* Garnet or aluminum oxide is best. They cost more but last longer than flint. You will need 60, 80, 100 and 150 grit for sanding the wood and some finer wet or dry sandpaper for the finish later. Sandpaper sheets come 9-inch by 11-inch sheets and can be cut to 3-inch by 3½-inch pieces, to get nine pieces from each sheet.

• *Small nails or brads.* If you choose to nail the parts together, use nails 1½-inch long or shorter.

• *Paints, stains and wax.* See page 5 for information on finishing the banks. Be extra careful to use non-toxic finishing materials because these banks will draw the attention of small children who love to put things in their mouths. Food color diluted in water makes excellent stain in a variety of colors. Wax in paste form is a good finish material. Mineral oil or vegetable oil is also good for the hand-rubbed look.

• *Enlarging patterns.* In some cases, the patterns in this book will need to be enlarged to make the bank exactly as it appears in the photograph. The easiest way to enlarge the patterns is to use a photocopier or a computer. The percentages by which the patterns need to be enlarged are indicated on the pattern. The patterns are laid out so that when enlarged, everything on one 8½-inch by 11-inch piece of paper will fit on a 17-inch by 11-inch piece of paper.

Templates make it easy to lay out the bank parts. Be sure to position the parts so the grain runs in the same direction for each piece.

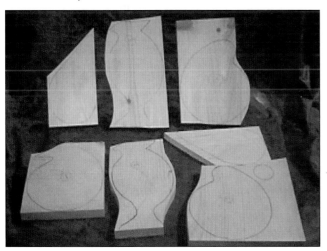

Cut the pieces down to size and then saw them to shape. It is easier to saw smaller shapes than to work with a large board.

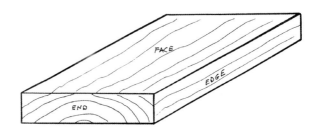

Illustration 1
Each board has six sides: two faces, two ends and two edges.

Construction Tips

All the banks in this book are constructed using the laminating process. This means the banks are built up by gluing the surfaces of the wood together. Pick up a rectangular piece of wood and notice that it has six surfaces. (See Illus. 1) The **face** is the large flat surface, sometimes called the top or bottom. The **edge** is the narrow surface, running the length of the board on each side. The grain is fairly straight. The **end** is the section that shows the tree's growth rings.

These six surfaces have different grain characteristics, and grain is very important in working with wood. You may glue any of these surfaces together except the end grain. If you try to glue the end grain you will have a very weak joint. The banks in this book are made by gluing the wood together face to face to create a block of laminated wood as the bank you are making requires. If the faces of the boards are smooth and flat or straight, you can glue the parts together without clamps, using yellow glue. If the boards are warped or cupped, you will have to clamp the parts flat until the glue sets (about one hour for yellow glue and about four or more hours for white glue).

If you are going to make more than one bank—and you probably will, because everyone who sees one will say, "Oh, would you make me one?"—take the time to make cardboard templates for the parts. You can save a lot of time if you have templates to trace.

When you have the full-size pattern, the next step is to lay out each part on the wood. This step must be carried out with care and planning. The grain must run in the same direction on each piece to give maximum strength. Avoid knots or position the pattern so the knot is hidden.

Use a pencil to trace around the templates. Pencil marks are easy to sand off or erase; ink soaks in and could spoil the look of the finished bank. (I used a soft-tipped marker for extra contrast in the photographs.)

Cutting

Once the parts are laid out, cut them out to shape and size. You can use a scroll saw, a band saw or a coping saw.

If you are using a **scroll saw,** you'll want to cut most pieces individually before gluing them together. Many scroll saws will have a tough time cutting the thicker layered parts.

Cut each part out as close to the lines as you can, but be sure to leave the line showing. If you cut the line off you will have no reference point when filing or sanding. (I have seen some funny-looking parts when students took the line off and kept on sanding, completely changing the shape of their projects.)

When the parts are cut out, examine them and see if you need to correct any cuts. Sometimes it is easier to true up a cut before assembly. If you wait until later the parts will be in hard-to-work positions. The rooster is an example of this. The heart, turtle, and owl banks are all easier to smooth out after the body is glued up.

If you are using a **coping saw,** keep the saw at a 90-degree angle from the surface to make a square edge. Saw with a smooth back-and-forth motion. Do not use very much pressure or you will break a lot of

The scroll saw works well for cutting the outside shapes and for removing the inside areas.

blades and get a very rough cut. Try to get a feel for how the saw wants to cut and you will have smooth edges. Care in sawing saves a lot of time and effort later during the filing and sanding stages.

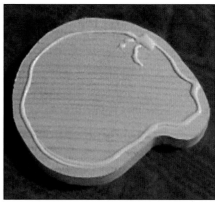

Use glue around the outer edges of the parts. Yellow carpenter's glue will dry faster than white glue.

If you are using a **band saw,** it may be easier to glue up the pieces first and then cut out the shapes. For example, the owl bank can be glued up first. Glue the two center body pieces together; then cut the middle out. Next, glue the outer pieces to the center. Cut the outside shape all at once.

A starter hole may not always be necessary when you are cutting out the area to hold the coins. Usually, you can cut in from the outside through the coin slot. If this is not possible, drill a ½ in. hole through the piece. Take the blade out of the saw, insert it through the hole and replace the blade into the saw frame. When you have finished the cut, reverse the process. The blade can be turned in the frame to reach difficult areas.

Shaping

When the parts are glued together you can start smoothing the edges and getting the shape of the bank. I find that the best way to do this is with a fine-tooth patternmaker's wood rasp, half-round, 8-inch long; but you can also use a fine-tooth cabinet rasp. Some people may prefer to use a rotary tool. Take your time with the filing and shaping, as this is often what gives character to the bank. A little more off in one place, a lit-

Clamps hold the parts together until the glue dries.

tle less in another, and you can change the whole appearance of the bank.

After you have worked a while, stand back and look at the bank or get someone else's opinion. The

The belly of this bank figure is glued up and ready for legs. Note the slot in which money will be put.

better the job you do with the rasp, the less filing you will have to do. When you have rounded all the corners and have the shape you want, start with the cabinetmaker's file. File the rasp marks smooth. You can do a really good job with the cabinet file and again it will save on the sanding. (Some people like the rough texture of the rasp and go right from there to sanding.)

I usually start with 80-grit sandpaper after filing. If you have some rough spots you could not file out, use 60-grit sandpaper to sand them down. Next I use 100-grit and then 120-grit sandpaper. The surface will then usually be smooth enough for the finish. Remember, sand only with the grain. It will take about fifty strokes with the grain to remove the crossgrain scratches from one careless stroke across the grain.

Most of the eyes are made with a ½-inch spade-type bit. Drill about half an inch deep. This is a simple way to make an eye. You can also make eyes from dowels, chair buttons and such and glue them on. Remember, though, to avoid small parts that could cause a choking hazard to young children.

Coin Removal

Most of the banks require a 1½-inch-diameter hole drilled into the body for coin removal. This can best be done after the body is glued up, as it is easier to locate the hole then. Use a 1½-in. diameter hole saw in a ¼-in. electric drill to make this hole. Cut the plug that is pressed into this hole a little bit bigger than the hole.

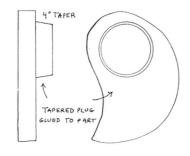

Sand it on a slight taper for a tight fit. A disc sander is very handy for this step. Sand at about a 4-degree angle.

The finished plug should only go about halfway into the hole without pressure. This

Set the disk sander table to 4 degrees to make the plugs.

will ensure a tight fit which will get looser with use. The plug is glued to the back of the part that will cover the hole. When dry, the part is used to twist the plug into the hole. This makes it a secret. Everyone will ask, "How do you get the money out?"

Finishing

I like a clear finish best for these banks as it shows off the natural beauty of the wood, but this is a personal choice. Sometimes I use different-colored woods are used to give contrast, such as mahogany with pine. A similar effect can be obtained with stain or paint. Again, be sure to use non-toxic stains and paints if the banks will be used by children.

Hand-rubbed oil or wax makes a very nice finish. Simply apply and rub with a soft cloth to a nice luster. If you use a clear finish, such as lacquer or varnish, apply as directed on the container. Use three or four thin coats and sand lightly between each with fine sandpaper (200-grit or finer). Apply a coat of wax and polish with a soft cloth.

If you choose to glue and nail your banks together, try to position the nails where they will not show. If a nail will show, "set it" by punching it below the surface. Using the point of another nail, insert a small amount of glue and sand over the hole immediately. The sawdust will mix into the glue and hide the hole, or at least make the nail less visible.

All the banks that are rectangular blocks with face-mounted parts, such as the Flower Bank on page 22, use the same body (pattern on page 80). You can make several bodies at one time and use them to create different banks.

Angel Bank

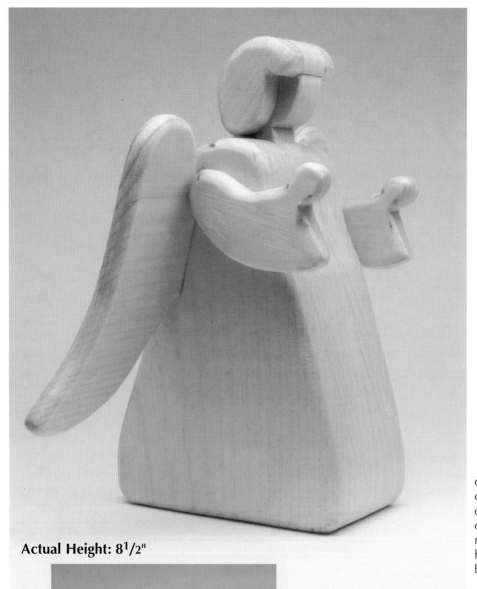

Actual Height: 8¹/₂"

Angels are popular these days. I find it interesting that our concept of angels is not even close to the biblical description of "fearsome warriors." Since most would not recognize them, here is my rendition of the angel bank.

Lay out the three center pieces: one on ³/₄-inch stock and two on ¹/₂-inch stock. Cut the parts to shape. Glue the center parts together and, when dry, cut out the coin slot. Keep the coin slot about ¹/₈-inch wide and straight, so the coins can enter but not fall out.

Lay out and cut the two side pieces from ¹/₂-inch stock. Glue the side pieces to the hollow centerpiece assembly. When the glue has set, drill a 1¹/₂-inch-diameter hole for coin removal over which the wings will be attached.

Cut the wings out of ¹/₂-inch stock. Cut the space for the wings to fit very tightly.

Lay out the two arms on ¹/₂-inch stock. Lay out the two hair pieces on ¹/₂-inch stock. Rasp and shape the hair to give it a rounded look. Glue these pieces to the assembly. Make the plug to fit the hole for coin removal and glue the plug to the back of the wings. The wings can also be secured with two screws.

Rasp, file and sand until the edges are smooth and the corners are nicely rounded. Apply the finish of your choice.

Angel Bank Pattern

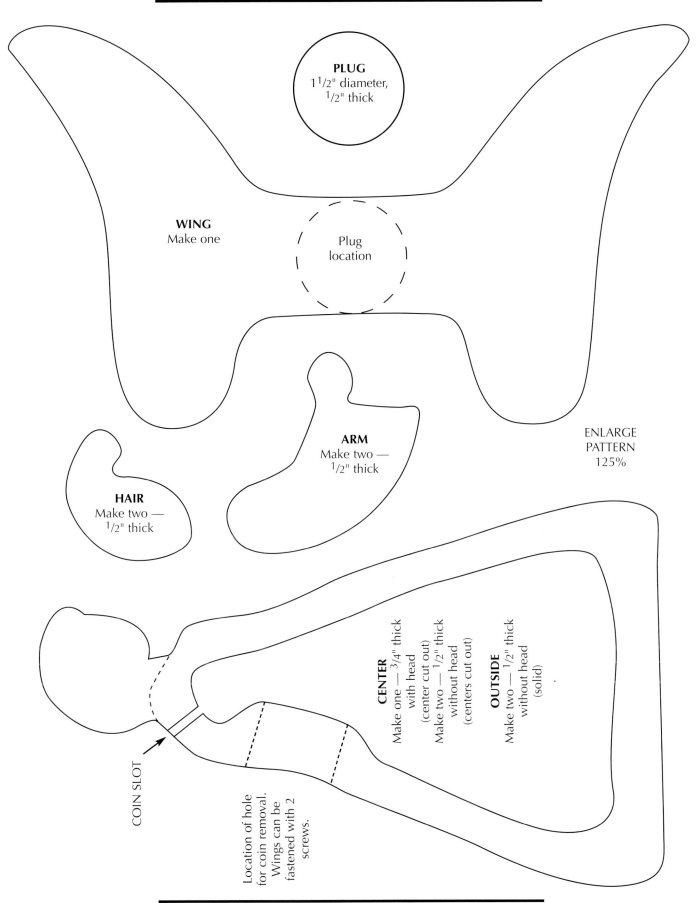

PLUG
1 1/2" diameter,
1/2" thick

WING
Make one

Plug
location

ENLARGE
PATTERN
125%

ARM
Make two —
1/2" thick

HAIR
Make two —
1/2" thick

CENTER
Make one — 3/4" thick
with head
(center cut out)
Make two — 1/2" thick
without head
(centers cut out)

OUTSIDE
Make two — 1/2" thick
without head
(solid)

COIN SLOT

Location of hole
for coin removal.
Wings can be
fastened with 2
screws.

Bear Bank

Actual Height: 8¹/₂"

When this book was first written I was teaching woodworking in Connecticut. We made actuated bears with doweled legs. One of my students suggested that I make a bear bank, and this is the result.

The bear bank is straightforward construction. It can be made in either of two ways.

Method 1: Cut the body pieces out and glue and clamp them together. Rasp and sand the entire body to shape. The body pieces are all the same, except the two outer pieces that have ears. Cut out the arms and legs and round the edges. Glue 1¹/₂-inch plugs to each arm, and 1¹/₂-inch plugs to each leg. Drill the 1¹/₂-inch holes to accept the arms and legs. Finish as desired. A dark brown walnut stain is good.

Method 2: Make the center of the body the usual way, but cut the outside pieces from several parts to make shaping them easier. The head and the body can be made with two side pieces. These can be cut out at an angle to eliminate some of the shaping by hand.

Bear Bank Pattern

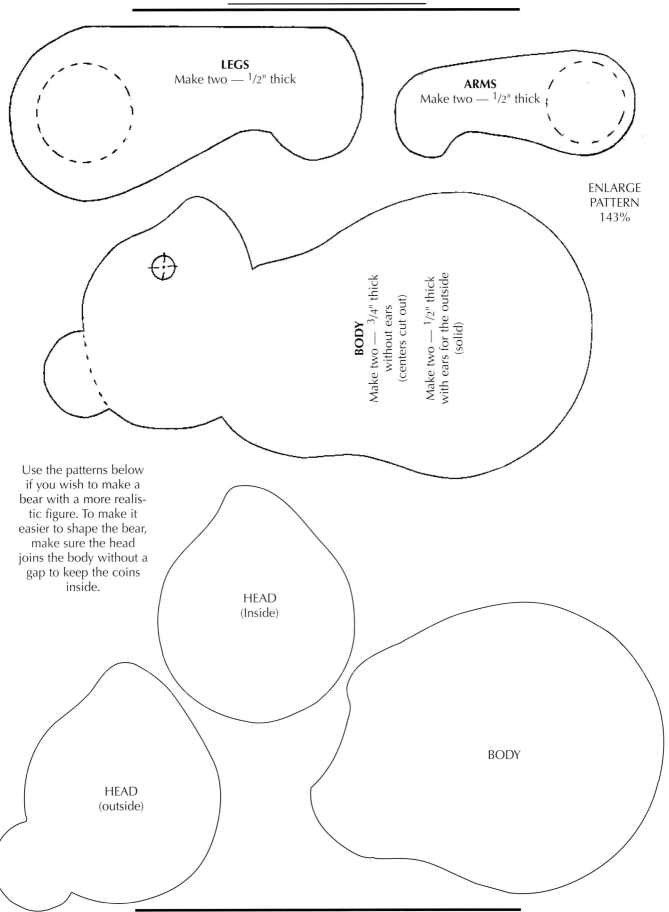

LEGS
Make two — 1/2" thick

ARMS
Make two — 1/2" thick

ENLARGE
PATTERN
143%

BODY
Make two — 3/4" thick
without ears
(centers cut out)

Make two — 1/2" thick
with ears for the outside
(solid)

Use the patterns below
if you wish to make a
bear with a more realis-
tic figure. To make it
easier to shape the bear,
make sure the head
joins the body without a
gap to keep the coins
inside.

HEAD
(Inside)

HEAD
(outside)

BODY

Bunny Bank

Actual Height: 4"

All the parts for this bank are made from $1/2$-inch-thick wood. Lay out the parts and cut them to shape. Note the direction of the grain on the ears and the legs. Glue the three middle pieces together, tail in the center.

Make a $1/8$-inch-wide coin slot between the ears and sand at this time, as it is quite difficult to sand when the sides are glued on. Glue the sides to the middle section. Drill two $1/2$-inch-diameter holes $1/8$-inch deep for the eyes. Drill a $1^1/2$-inch-diameter hole under one rear leg and glue the plug to the underside of this leg. Glue the three other legs to the body.

Rasp all the corners until they are round. Taper the nose toward the middle. Sand until smooth. Finish as desired.

Bunny Bank Pattern

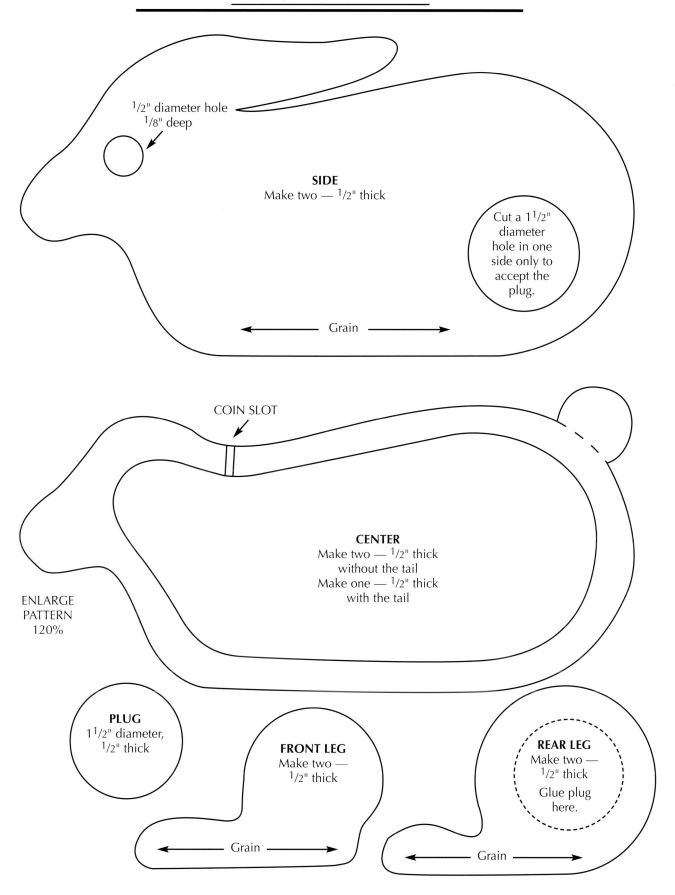

½" diameter hole
⅛" deep

SIDE
Make two — ½" thick

Cut a 1½" diameter hole in one side only to accept the plug.

Grain

COIN SLOT

CENTER
Make two — ½" thick
without the tail
Make one — ½" thick
with the tail

ENLARGE
PATTERN
120%

PLUG
1½" diameter,
½" thick

FRONT LEG
Make two —
½" thick

REAR LEG
Make two —
½" thick

Glue plug
here.

Grain

Grain

Cardinal Bank

Actual Height: 8"

This funny little bird was developed from a garden ornament.

Lay out the parts on the stock. Part 1 is ³/4-inch thick. Part 2 and Part 3 are ¹/2-inch thick.

Cut out the parts and glue the center section together. Cut the coin slot; then glue Part 3 to this assembly. Drill the eye holes about ¹/2-inch deep. Drill the 1¹/2-inch hole for coin removal. Shape the body parts to be smooth and nicely rounded.

Cut four foot pieces. Sand or cut the 45-degree angles. Glue them to each foot. Cut out the two wings and glue the plug on one wing. Glue the other wing to the side. Sand until smooth. Apply the finish of your choice.

Cardinal Bank Pattern

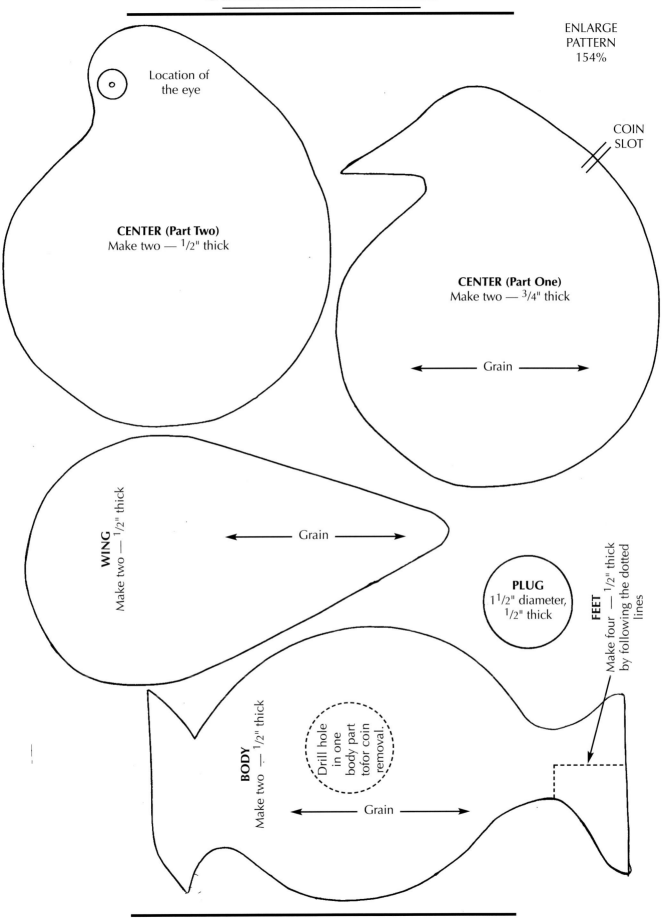

ENLARGE
PATTERN
154%

Location of
the eye

CENTER (Part Two)
Make two — 1/2" thick

COIN
SLOT

CENTER (Part One)
Make two — 3/4" thick

← Grain →

WING
Make two — 1/2" thick

← Grain →

PLUG
1 1/2" diameter,
1/2" thick

FEET — 1/2" thick
Make four
by following the dotted
lines

BODY
Make two — 1/2" thick

Drill hole
in one
body part
to for coin
removal.

← Grain →

Cat Bank

Actual Height: 9¹/₄"

Lay out the front and back of the cat on ³/₄-inch wood. Note the direction of the grain on these pieces. The body is made from four rings cut from ³/₄-inch-thick wood. The outside of the ring is a 3-inch-diameter circle. The center hole has a 2-inch diameter. Lay out these rings on the wood and use a 2-inch-diameter hole saw or scroll saw to remove the inside.

When the inside is removed, cut the outside to shape. Glue two rings together. When the glue has set, cut a ¹/₈-inch-wide coin slot across the side of these two rings into the center hole. Glue one additional ring on both ends of this assembly to form a 3-inch-long cylinder. Make a ¹/₂-inch-thick plug with a 2-inch diameter. Taper it slightly to fit tightly into one end of the cylinder. Glue this plug to either the front or the back of the cat. Glue the other piece (front or back) to the cylinder.

Rasp, file and sand until all edges are round and smooth. Use a soldering pencil to burn the eyes, nose, mouth and whiskers into the face. Finish as desired.

Cat Bank Pattern

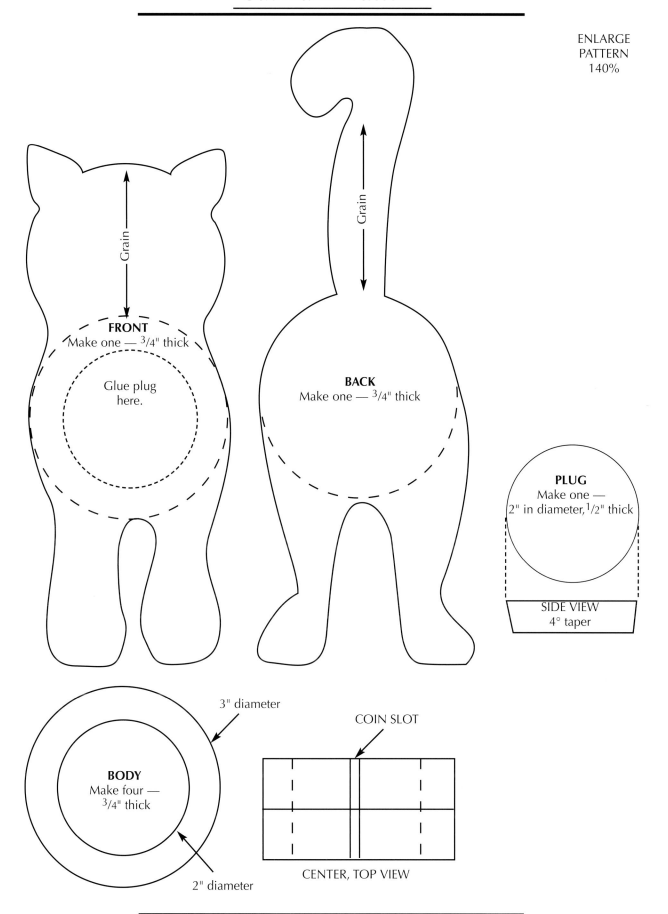

ENLARGE
PATTERN
140%

Grain

Grain

FRONT
Make one — 3/4" thick

Glue plug
here.

BACK
Make one — 3/4" thick

PLUG
Make one —
2" in diameter, 1/2" thick

SIDE VIEW
4° taper

3" diameter

BODY
Make four —
3/4" thick

2" diameter

COIN SLOT

CENTER, TOP VIEW

Clown Bank

Actual Height: 8¹/₄"

Use wood with contrasting colors to create the appearance of clown makeup. You could also use paint or stain to get the desired effect.

Lay out the parts and cut them to shape. Glue the two center sections together and saw out the middle, as indicated by the dotted line, to receive and hold the coins. Glue the back and the front to the two center pieces. File and sand the outside edges of this assembly to shape. Glue the face piece, mouth and hat brim in place.

File and sand the edges until round and smooth. Drill ¹/₂-inch-diameter holes ¹/₈-inch deep for the eyes. Drill a 1¹/₂-inch hole for the nose. Sand the nose, which acts as the plug, to a taper for a tight fit.

Clown Bank Pattern

COIN SLOT

FACE PIECE
Make one — 1/2" thick

Drill hole 1 1/2" diameter to accept nose plug.

CENTER, FRONT & BACK
Make two — 3/4" thick
(cut out centers)

Make two — 1/2" thick
(solid)

HAT BRIM
Make one — 1/2" thick

MOUTH
Make one — 1/2" thick

Cut out for mouth.

NOSE
Make one —
3/4" thick,
1 3/4" diameter

Taper to 1 1/2" to fit hole in face.

ENLARGE PATTERN 153%

Elephant Bank

Actual Height: 5³/4"

Lay out the face, front and back on ¹/2-inch-thick wood. Lay out the leg and body pieces on ³/4-inch-thick stock. Cut all the parts to shape. Glue the two ³/4-inch-thick body pieces together. Cut a ¹/8-inch-wide coin slot across the top into the center cavity.

Glue the ¹/2-inch pieces to the front and back of the center assembly. Glue the leg pieces on front and back so that one set is to the left and the other to the right. Drill a 1¹/2-inch-diameter hole under the center of the head into the body cavity. Drill ¹/2–inch-wide holes ¹/8-inch deep with a spade bit for eyes. Glue a 1¹/2-inch-diameter tapered plug to the back of the head.

File and sand round and smooth. Apply finish as desired.

Elephant Bank Pattern

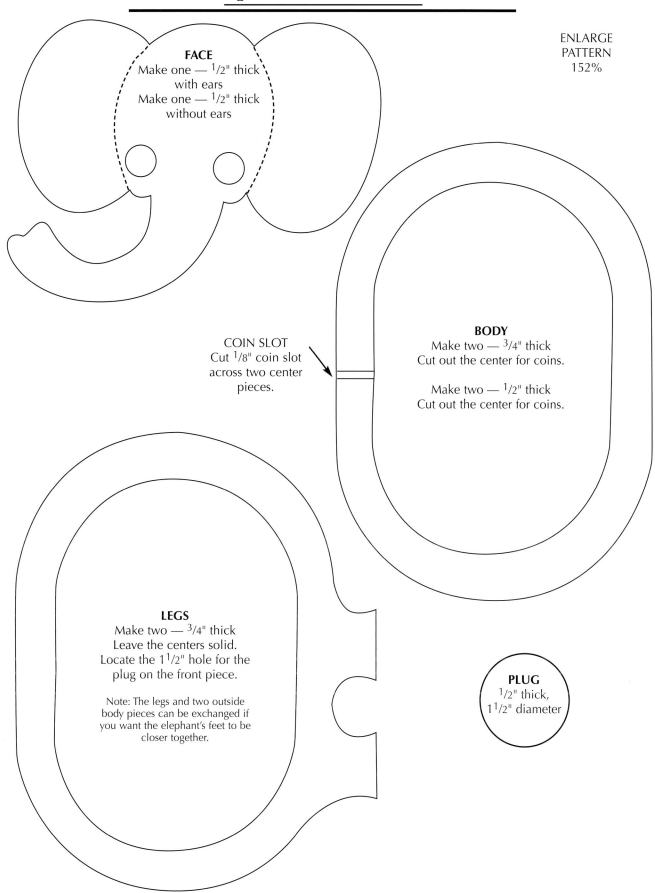

FACE
Make one — $1/2"$ thick
with ears
Make one — $1/2"$ thick
without ears

ENLARGE
PATTERN
152%

COIN SLOT
Cut $1/8"$ coin slot
across two center
pieces.

BODY
Make two — $3/4"$ thick
Cut out the center for coins.

Make two — $1/2"$ thick
Cut out the center for coins.

LEGS
Make two — $3/4"$ thick
Leave the centers solid.
Locate the $1^1/2"$ hole for the
plug on the front piece.

Note: The legs and two outside
body pieces can be exchanged if
you want the elephant's feet to be
closer together.

PLUG
$1/2"$ thick,
$1^1/2"$ diameter

Gray Elephant Bank

Actual Height: 5"

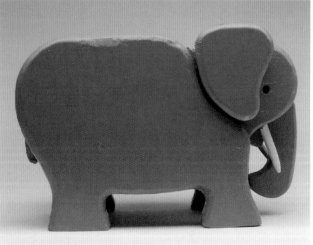

Lay out the parts on 3/4-inch-thick wood and cut them to shape. The trunk and legs should be filed and sanded round and smooth before assembly. Drill holes under the location of the ears. Make two 1 1/2-inch-diameter tapered plugs to fit tightly into these holes and glue them to the back of the ears. Drill 1/4-inch holes to hold 1/4-inch by 1 1/2-inch-long dowels for the tusks. Glue the parts together.

File and sand all edges round and smooth. Apply finish as desired.

Gray Elephant Bank Pattern

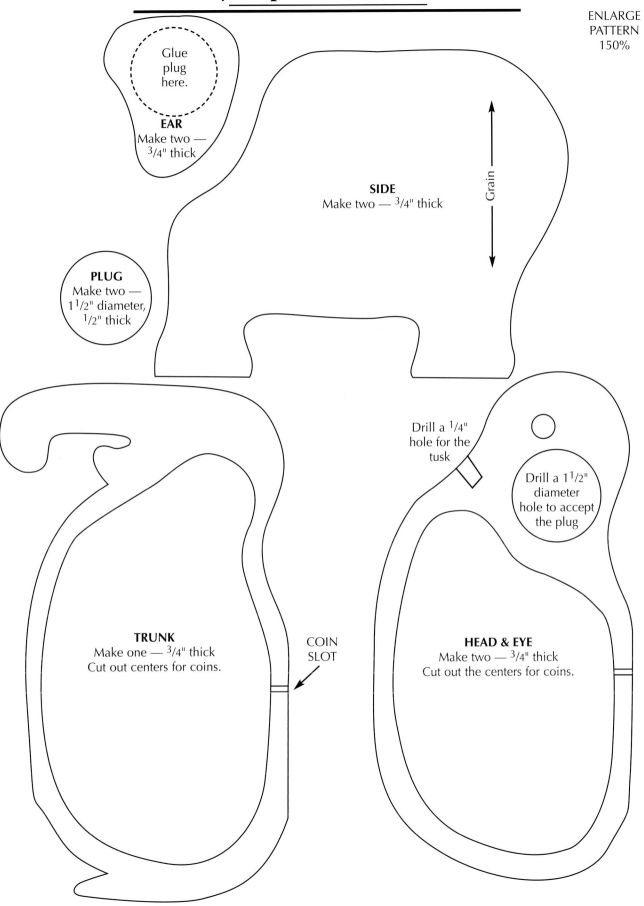

ENLARGE
PATTERN
150%

Glue
plug
here.

EAR
Make two —
3/4" thick

SIDE
Make two — 3/4" thick

Grain

PLUG
Make two —
1 1/2" diameter,
1/2" thick

Drill a 1/4"
hole for the
tusk

Drill a 1 1/2"
diameter
hole to accept
the plug

TRUNK
Make one — 3/4" thick
Cut out centers for coins.

COIN
SLOT

HEAD & EYE
Make two — 3/4" thick
Cut out the centers for coins.

Flower Bank

Actual Height: 8¹/₂"

The rectangular-backed banks are easy to create and the design possibilities are endless. Experiment with different shapes or give the banks square corners to create other variations.

Use the pattern on page 80 to create the rectangular box for the coins. Cut two pieces of ³/₄-inch stock with the middles cut out for the center of the box. Cut two pieces ¹/₈-inch plywood for the front and back. The front and back pieces can also be made of thicker stock if you desire a thicker bank. Glue and clamp the pieces together.

Cut out the flower parts; then sand and stain before gluing them to the face of the bank. Make the flowers red or yellow, the leaves and stem green, and the flower pot brown. The hole and plug for removing coins are behind the flower. The top corner of the round part of the flower should be rasped heavily to make it quite round.

Flower Bank Pattern

PATTERN
100%

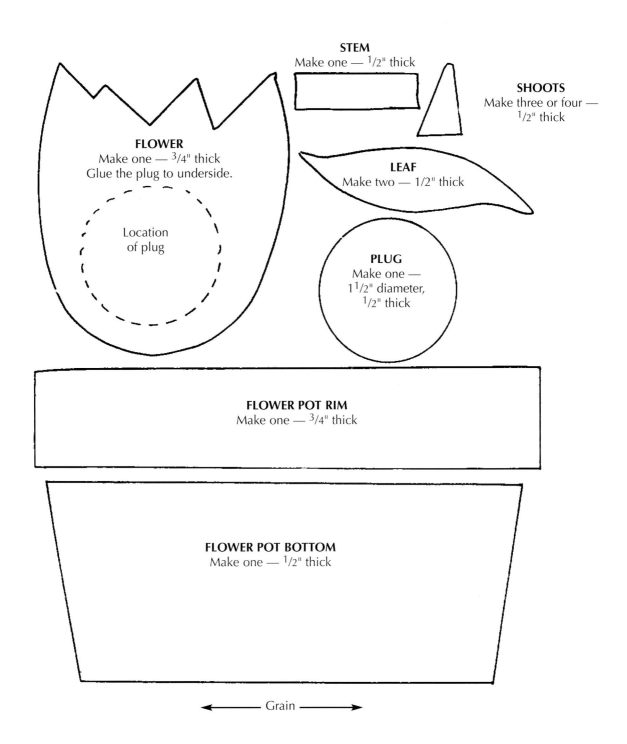

STEM
Make one — $^1/_2$" thick

SHOOTS
Make three or four —
$^1/_2$" thick

FLOWER
Make one — $^3/_4$" thick
Glue the plug to underside.

Location
of plug

LEAF
Make two — 1/2" thick

PLUG
Make one —
$1^1/_2$" diameter,
$^1/_2$" thick

FLOWER POT RIM
Make one — $^3/_4$" thick

FLOWER POT BOTTOM
Make one — $^1/_2$" thick

← Grain →

Hole in One Bank

Actual Height: 8¹/₂"

This bank is for all the golfers that never got a "Hole-in One!"

Use the pattern on page 80 to create the rectangular box for the coins. Cut two pieces of ³/₄-inch stock with the middles cut out for the center of the box. Cut two pieces ¹/₂-inch stock for the front and back. The front and back pieces can also be made of ¹/₈-inch plywood if you desire a thinner bank. Glue and clamp the pieces together. Drill a 1¹/₂-inch hole for coin removal into the hollow through the bottom of this assembly.

Cut out the No. 1 from ¹/₂-inch stock, and drill a hole through the middle. Rout or sand the edges until it is nicely rounded. Glue the No. 1 to the middle of the box.

Cut out the freeform base from ³/₄-inch stock. Round the edges. Fasten the base to the bottom of the bank with two 1¹/₂-inch dry wall screws. (The screws will need to be removed and the base taken off to take out the money.) Drill a hole through the base and screw the golf ball down with a 1¹/₂-inch dry wall screw.

Paint or stain the base green and apply a clear finish.

Hole in One Bank Pattern

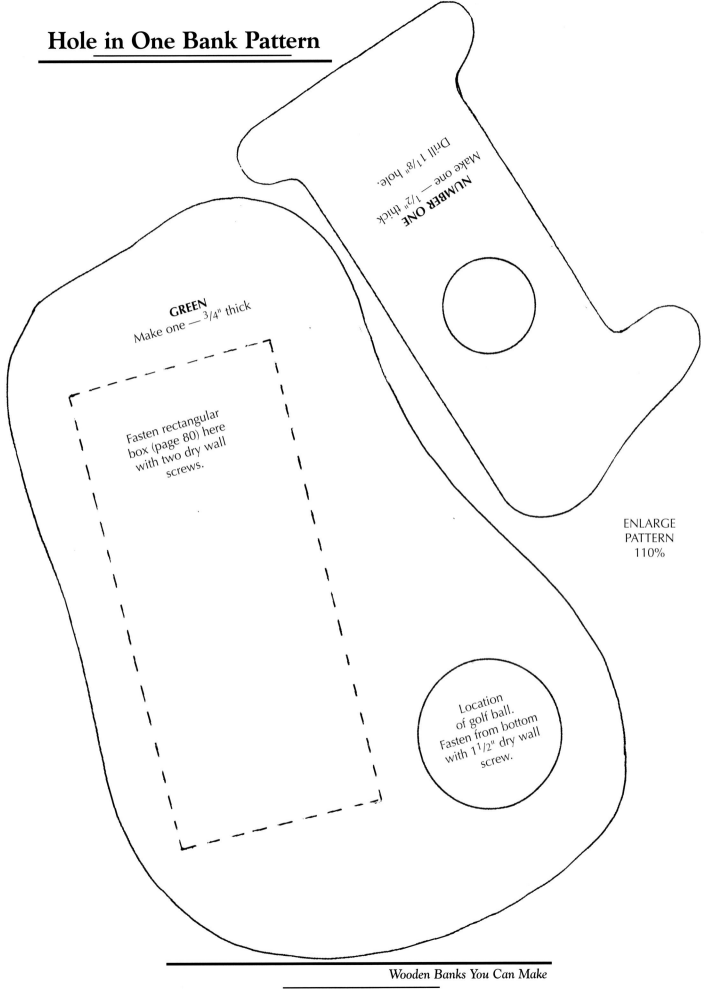

GREEN
Make one — 3/4" thick

Fasten rectangular box (page 80) here with two dry wall screws.

NUMBER ONE
Make one — 1/2" thick
Drill 1 1/8" hole.

ENLARGE PATTERN 110%

Location of golf ball. Fasten from bottom with 1 1/2" dry wall screw.

Heart Bank

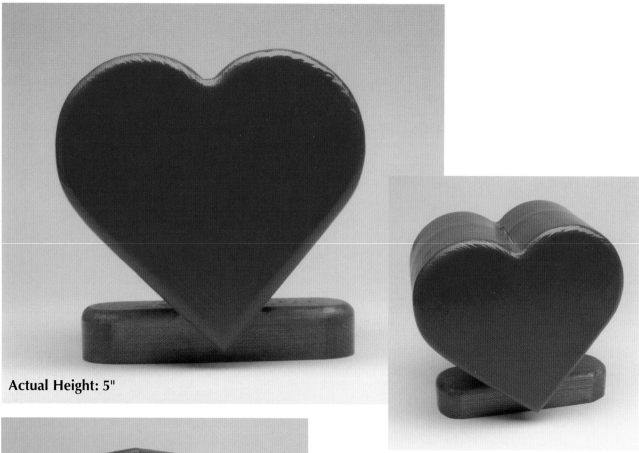

Actual Height: 5"

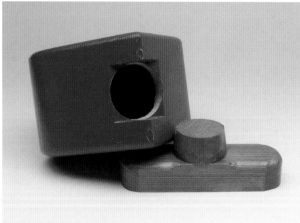

Begin construction of the heart by laying out the five parts on $1/2$-inch and $3/4$-inch stock. On the front and back piece, the grain must run vertically so the points will not break when the base is inserted between them. The grain also runs the length of the base.

Cut the parts to shape. Glue the two center parts together and, when dry, cut out the center, starting at the coin slot at the top. Keep the coin slot about $1/8$-inch wide and straight, so the coins can enter but not fall out. Glue the front and back pieces to the hollow center assembly. (Note: If you want a thinner bank you can use $1/8$-inch-thick pieces for the front and the back, but the center must be $1 1/2$-inch-thick to take the coins.) When the glue has set, drill a $1 1/2$-inch-diameter hole between the two points of the heart and into the cavity for coin removal.

Make the base piece slightly oversize. Sand it to fit tightly between the two points. Rasp, file and sand until the edges are smooth and the corners nicely rounded. Apply the finish of your choice.

Heart Bank Pattern

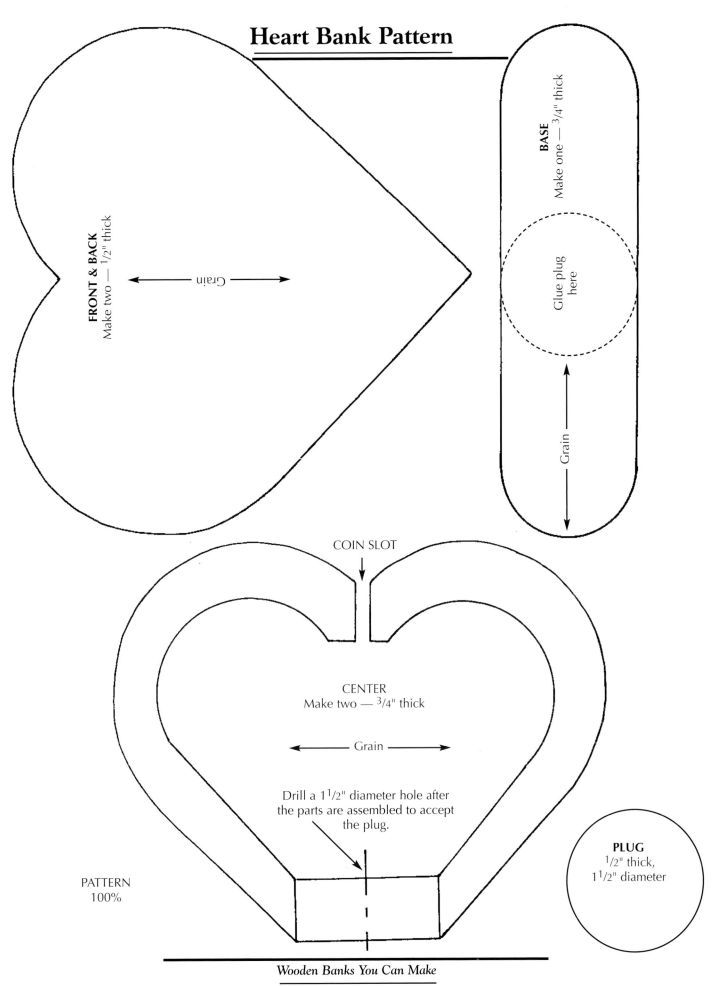

FRONT & BACK
Make two — 1/2" thick

← Grain →

BASE
Make one — 3/4" thick

Glue plug here

Grain

COIN SLOT

CENTER
Make two — 3/4" thick

← Grain →

Drill a 1 1/2" diameter hole after the parts are assembled to accept the plug.

PATTERN 100%

PLUG
1/2" thick,
1 1/2" diameter

Native American Bank

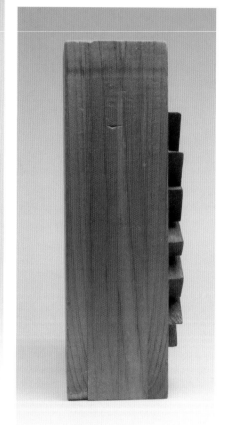

Actual Height: 8¹/2"

Notice that I do not call this an "Indian" bank. Native American fits much better.

Use the pattern on page 80 to create the rectangular box for the coins. Cut two pieces of ³/4-inch stock with the middles cut out for the center of the box. Cut two pieces ¹/2-inch stock for the front and back. The front and back pieces can also be made of ¹/8-inch plywood if you desire a thinner bank. Glue and clamp the pieces together.

Cut out the rest of the pieces from ¹/4-inch wood and glue them to the face of the bank. These pieces should be cut from darker wood for contrast. You may also choose to stain or paint them before gluing them the face of the rectangular box. Drill a 1¹/2-inch hole for coin removal. Make the 1¹/2-inch tapered plug from ³/4-inch stock.

Sand and finish as desired.

Native American Bank Pattern

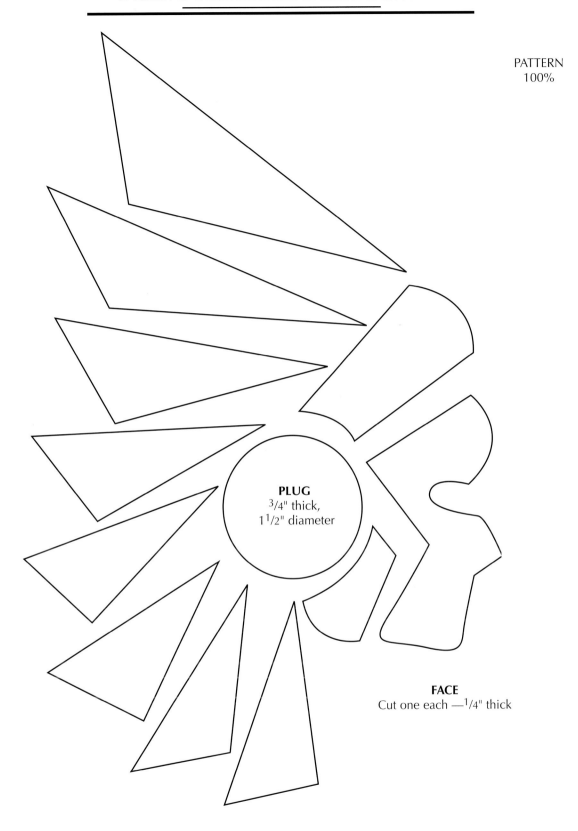

PLUG
3/4" thick,
1$^{1}/_{2}$" diameter

FACE
Cut one each —$^{1}/_{4}$" thick

Lion Bank

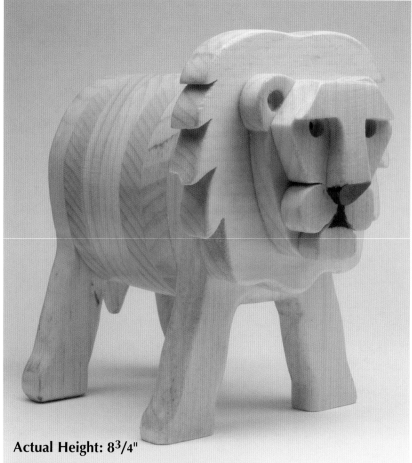

Actual Height: 8³/₄"

Use pine for this bank. It has a straw or light yellow color and works well for a lion.

The front and rear legs are the same pattern and are made of ³/₄-inch-thick wood. Make sure the grain is running the length of the legs for strength. Locate and drill a 1¹/₂-inch-diameter hole on both pieces for the head and tail plugs.

Cut out the five body pieces from ³/₄-inch stock. Glue and clamp two of the body pieces together to make one piece 1¹/₂ inches thick. Cut the ¹/₈-inch-wide coin slot through to the center.

Glue and clamp the legs and body pieces together being careful to position the coin slot in the center of the top. Make sure the bottoms of the legs are even so the lion will stand on a flat surface.

Lay out the mane on a piece of ³/₄-inch wood and carefully cut it to shape. Lay out the face and head on ¹/₂-inch stock and cut them out. Drill holes for the ears and eyes. Sand the ears with a piece of sand paper over your thumb, using a twisting motion to make them concave.

Shape the nose piece by sanding or filing a taper from the eyebrows to the nose; then back from the tip of the nose to the edge. The eyebrows should be about ¹/₈-inch thick. The nose comes to a point. Use black paint to color the tip of the nose and the triangle below the nose that forms the cheeks and chin. When the paint is dry, slightly round all the edges. Glue and clamp the three headpieces and the mane together.

The plugs are next. Cut the tail piece from ¹/₂-inch stock. Glue and clamp one plug to the tail. To line up the head on the body, place the other plug loosely in the hole and coat it with glue. Next, line up the head and touch it to the wet glue on the plug. Lift it the head off and you will have a wet circle of glue in the exact location to make the head look correct. Often the plug will come off with the head when you lift it. Just make sure it is in the right position and clamp it.

Apply a clear coat of finish, stain or paint as desired.

Lion Bank—Pattern

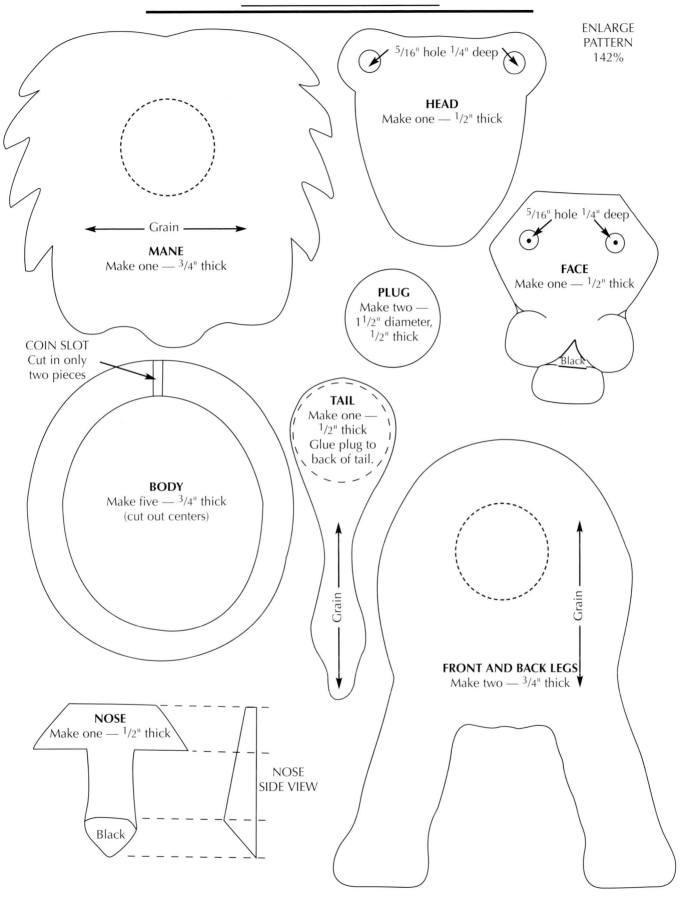

ENLARGE
PATTERN
142%

5/16" hole 1/4" deep

HEAD
Make one — 1/2" thick

MANE
Make one — 3/4" thick

Grain

5/16" hole 1/4" deep

FACE
Make one — 1/2" thick

Black

PLUG
Make two —
1 1/2" diameter,
1/2" thick

COIN SLOT
Cut in only
two pieces

TAIL
Make one —
1/2" thick
Glue plug to
back of tail.

BODY
Make five — 3/4" thick
(cut out centers)

Grain

FRONT AND BACK LEGS
Make two — 3/4" thick

Grain

NOSE
Make one — 1/2" thick

NOSE
SIDE VIEW

Black

Monocle Man Bank

Actual Height: 8¹/2"

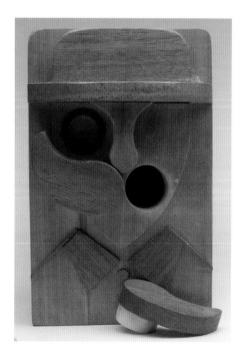

I can't remember how this bank came into being. But it's a good one, so I keep making it.

The pattern for the rectangular box that forms the base of this bank is on page 80. Cut two pieces of ³/4-inch stock with the middles cut out for the center of the box. Cut two pieces ¹/2-inch stock for the front and back. The front and back pieces can also be made of ¹/8-inch plywood if you desire a thinner bank. Glue and clamp the pieces together.

Cut out the rest of the pieces out of ¹/2-inch stock and glue them to the face of the bank. The collar should be made of thin wood about ¹/4-inch thick. You can cut out one collar piece of ¹/2-inch stock and then saw it through the middle to make two pieces. I use a thin-kerf Japanese saw for this.

Drill two 1¹/4-inch holes for coin removal behind where the mustache pieces will be located. Note that the normal size for these holes would be 1¹/2 inches thick, but that would make the mustache too big. Therefore, this bank will take coins up to a quarter; it will not allow half dollar coins to be removed, but I have not seen too many of those lately. Make the 1¹/4-inch tapered plugs and glue them to the back of the mustache pieces.

Sand and finish as desired.

Monocle Man Bank—Pattern

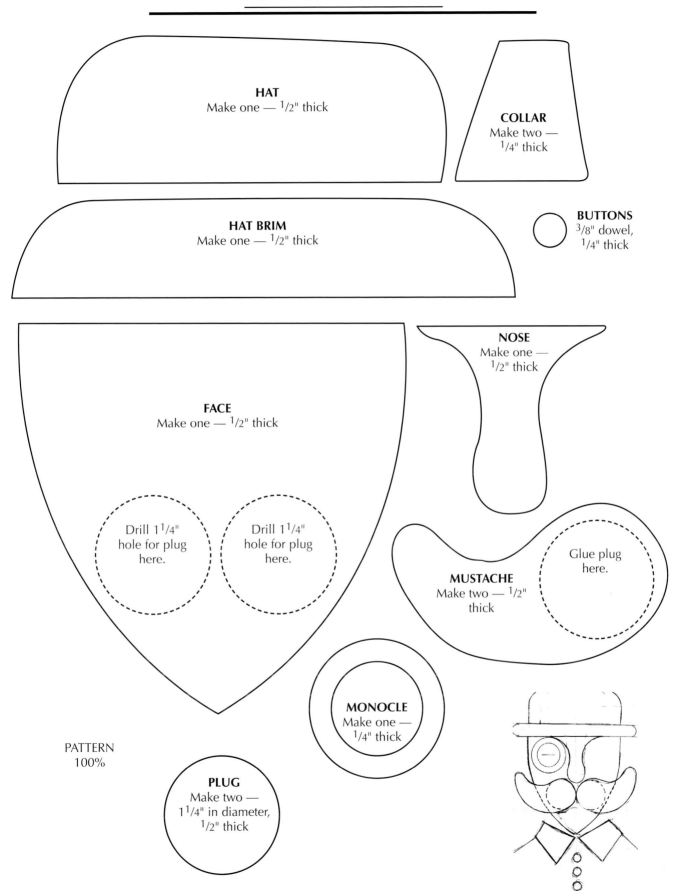

HAT
Make one — 1/2" thick

COLLAR
Make two —
1/4" thick

HAT BRIM
Make one — 1/2" thick

BUTTONS
3/8" dowel,
1/4" thick

NOSE
Make one —
1/2" thick

FACE
Make one — 1/2" thick

Drill 1 1/4"
hole for plug
here.

Drill 1 1/4"
hole for plug
here.

Glue plug
here.

MUSTACHE
Make two — 1/2"
thick

MONOCLE
Make one —
1/4" thick

PATTERN
100%

PLUG
Make two —
1 1/4" in diameter,
1/2" thick

Music Note Bank

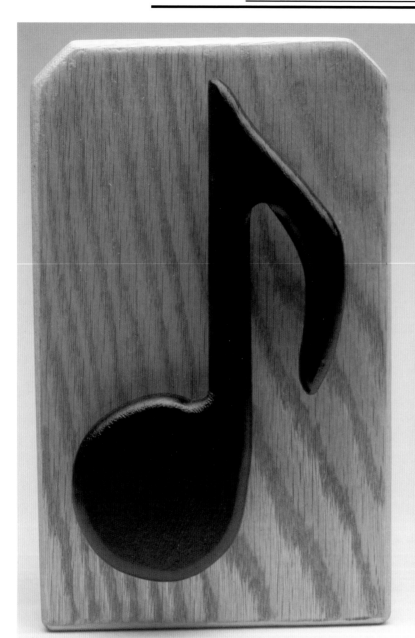

Actual Height: 8^1/$_2$"

This bank uses the same body as the other rectangular banks in this book. (See the pattern on page 80.)

Make the rectangular box following the directions on the pattern. The front, or background, of the box should be a light color for contrast. Drill a 1^1/$_2$-inch-diameter hole through the front into the cavity under the round part of the note.

Cut out the note from ^{1}/$_2$-inch stock. The note should be made of a strong hardwood or high-grade plywood for strength. File and sand the edges. Paint the note black. Glue the tapered plug to the back of the note.

Sand the bank smooth and finish as desired.

Music Note Bank—Pattern

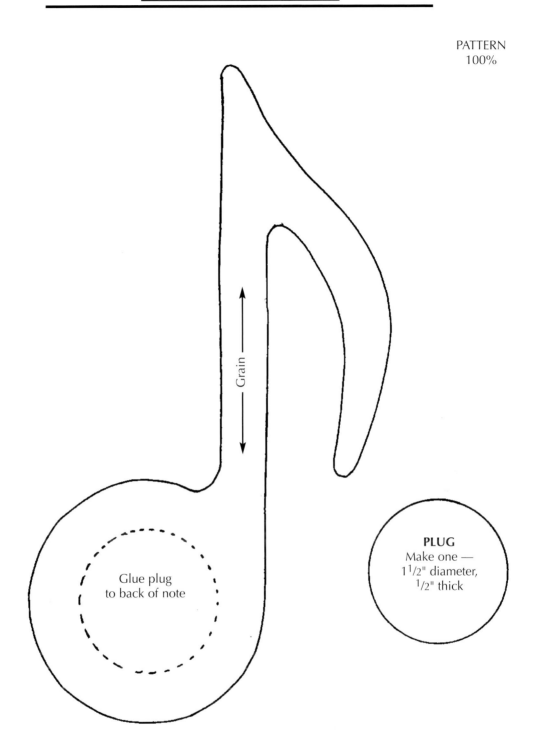

Grain

Glue plug
to back of note

PLUG
Make one —
1$\frac{1}{2}$" diameter,
$\frac{1}{2}$" thick

Owl Bank

Actual Height: 8"

This bank was made for my sister Nancy, who was hospitalized at the time for treatment of cancer. Owls were a favorite of hers.

This is a very simple bank to cut out and laminate. You will need about one square foot each of $3/4$-inch-thick and $1/2$-inch-thick stock. Any type of wood will work, including plywood. The use of contrasting colors makes it interesting. Pay attention to the direction of the grain to get the most strength and the most pleasing appearance of the parts.

Begin by tracing or gluing the body patterns onto the $3/4$-inch stock. Cut out these two pieces and glue them together. Cut the $1/8$-inch-wide by $1^1/2$-inch-long coin slot to receive the coins. Next cut two more pieces from $1/2$-inch-thick wood for the front and back. Glue them to the center section. This will make a closed box.

Cut out the eyes, side, wing and beak from $1/2$-inch wood. Sand the edges of these parts now to remove all saw marks. (Note: If you are using a top of the line saw with a good blade, there is no need to sand.) Glue these parts in place on the body of the owl. Sand the outside of the bank to smooth out the edges of the laminated pieces

and to give a good, pleasing shape to the owl. All areas should be rounded over.

Locate the center of the pupil of each eye and mark it with an awl. Drill the eye with a $1^1/2$-inch hole saw, $1/8$-inch deep. Drill the pupil with a $1/2$-inch spade bit.

Locate and drill a $1^1/2$ inch hole through the side and front piece into the cavity for the removal of the money. This hole is centered under where the top of the wing will be. You can use a spade bit or a forstner bit.

Cut a $1^1/2$ inch diameter plug from $1/2$-inch wood. This plug is cut or sanded at about a 4-degree angle. When lightly pressed into the hole in the side it should stand about $1/8$-inch proud of the surface. Glue the plug in place on the back of the wing. When the wing is twisted and pressed down the plug should tightly close and hide the hole.

Sand everything smooth, then finish the bank as desired. The surface can be stained or painted in colors to look like an owl. You can also choose to spray or brush on several coats of clear lacquer and let the natural beauty of the wood show.

Owl Bank—Pattern

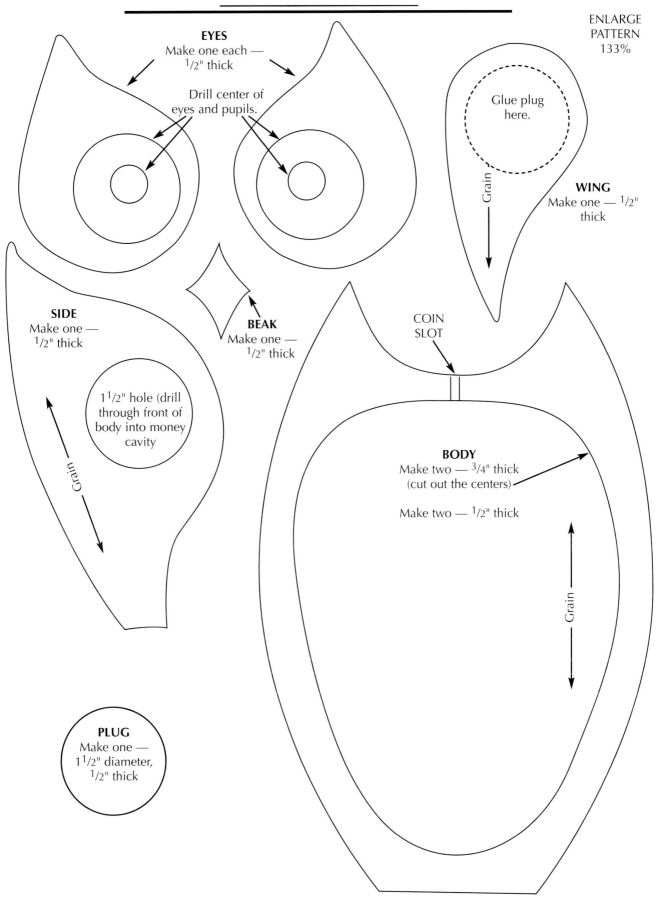

ENLARGE PATTERN 133%

EYES
Make one each —
1/2" thick

Drill center of eyes and pupils.

Glue plug here.

WING
Make one — 1/2" thick

Grain

SIDE
Make one —
1/2" thick

BEAK
Make one —
1/2" thick

COIN SLOT

1 1/2" hole (drill through front of body into money cavity

Grain

BODY
Make two — 3/4" thick
(cut out the centers)

Make two — 1/2" thick

Grain

PLUG
Make one —
1 1/2" diameter,
1/2" thick

Panda Bank

Actual Height: 6"

This is another very easy to make bank. Pandas are very popular these days. We even have a word, "Pandemonium," as a result of their popularity.

Start with the body. Draw or trace the two body parts (Part A) on to $3/4$-inch wood. They are actually 4-inch-diameter circles, with 3-inch-diameter circles cut out of the middle. The front and back body parts (Part B) need to have a C-shaped hole cut out of the center. A circular hole would allow the money to fall out between the legs. Glue the two body pieces together and, when set, cut the coin slot to the inside.

The front and back legs (Part C) are cut from $3/4$-inch stock. Drill a $1^1/2$-inch hole in the front legs for the plug that holds the head and allows access to the money. Sand the legs finish them with black paint before gluing them to the body assembly. Glue the legs and body assembly together.

The head is made up of four layers of $1/2$-inch wood. Part D (2 pieces) is the head and ears, Part E is the neck and Part F is the face. Cut out the eye sockets in the front piece. The eyes are $3/8$-inch holes drilled $1/4$-inch deep into the second piece. The third piece is the ear piece. Paint the ears black before gluing up the head. This will keep paint from getting on the other parts and making a mess. Cut out the nose and paint it black; then glued it on the front piece. Glue together all of the head pieces, including the tapered plug. Shape the bottom of the chin back toward the neck to make it look more like a panda's head.

Sand until smooth. Apply a clear coat of finish.

Panda Bank—Pattern

ENLARGE
PATTERN
133%

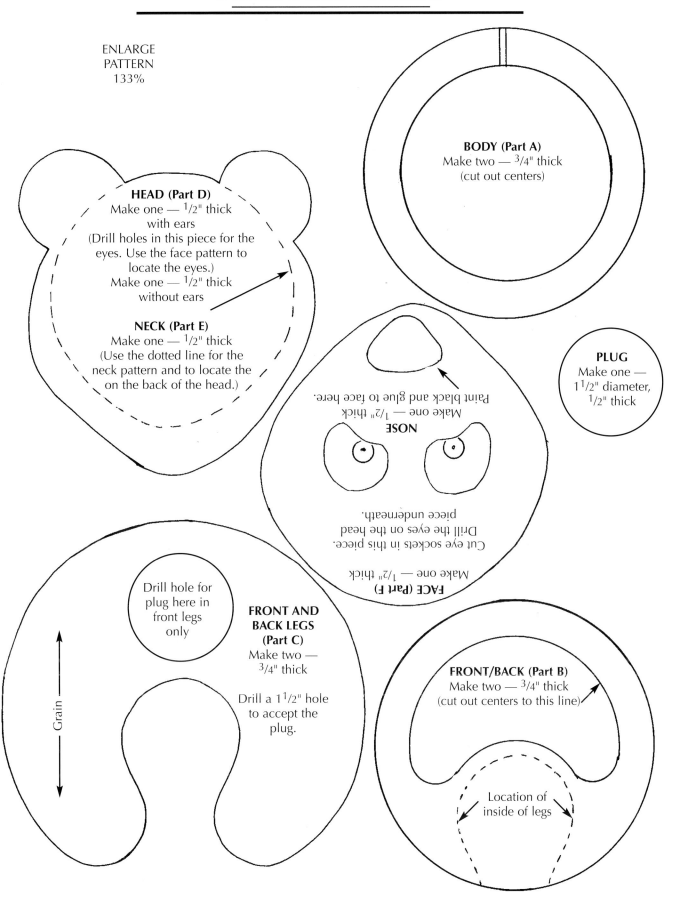

BODY (Part A)
Make two — 3/4" thick
(cut out centers)

HEAD (Part D)
Make one — 1/2" thick
with ears
(Drill holes in this piece for the
eyes. Use the face pattern to
locate the eyes.)
Make one — 1/2" thick
without ears

NECK (Part E)
Make one — 1/2" thick
(Use the dotted line for the
neck pattern and to locate the
on the back of the head.)

PLUG
Make one —
1 1/2" diameter,
1/2" thick

Paint black and glue to face here.

NOSE
Make one — 1/2" thick

Drill the eyes on the head
piece underneath.
Cut eye sockets in this piece.
Make one — 1/2" thick
FACE (Part F)

Drill hole for
plug here in
front legs
only

**FRONT AND
BACK LEGS
(Part C)**
Make two —
3/4" thick

Drill a 1 1/2" hole
to accept the
plug.

Grain

FRONT/BACK (Part B)
Make two — 3/4" thick
(cut out centers to this line)

Location of
inside of legs

Piggy Bank

Actual Height: 4^1/$_2$"

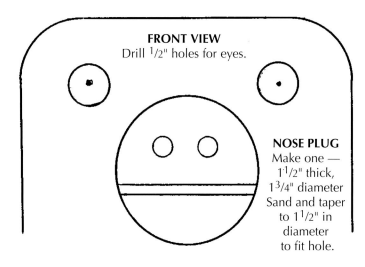

I modified my original piggy bank to make coin removal easier. In this new bank, the coins can be removed when the nose is removed.

Lay out the two center sections on ^{3}/4-inch stock. Cut out the centers to hold the coins. Glue these two pieces together and, when dry, cut a ^{1}/8-inch coin slot in the top to reach the coin chamber.

Lay out the feet parts on ^{3}/4-inch stock. Cut out the inside oval for the coin chamber. Glue these pieces to the center assembly. Be careful to get the feet even so the bank will stand flat on a dresser or desk top.

Lay out the two side pieces on ^{1}/2-inch stock. (If you want a fatter pig, try using ^{3}/4-inch stock instead). Glue the sides to the assembly.

Drill a 1^1/2-inch hole in through the front into the coin chamber to receive the nose. Glue two pieces of ^{3}/4-inch stock together to make a 1^1/2-inch block for the nose. Draw a 1^3/4-inch circle on the top of this block. Cut the circle out at a four degree angle. This will create the nose plug.

Sand until rounded and smooth. Finish as desired.

FRONT VIEW
Drill ^{1}/2" holes for eyes.

NOSE PLUG
Make one —
1^1/2" thick,
1^3/4" diameter
Sand and taper
to 1^1/2" in
diameter
to fit hole.

Piggy Bank—Pattern

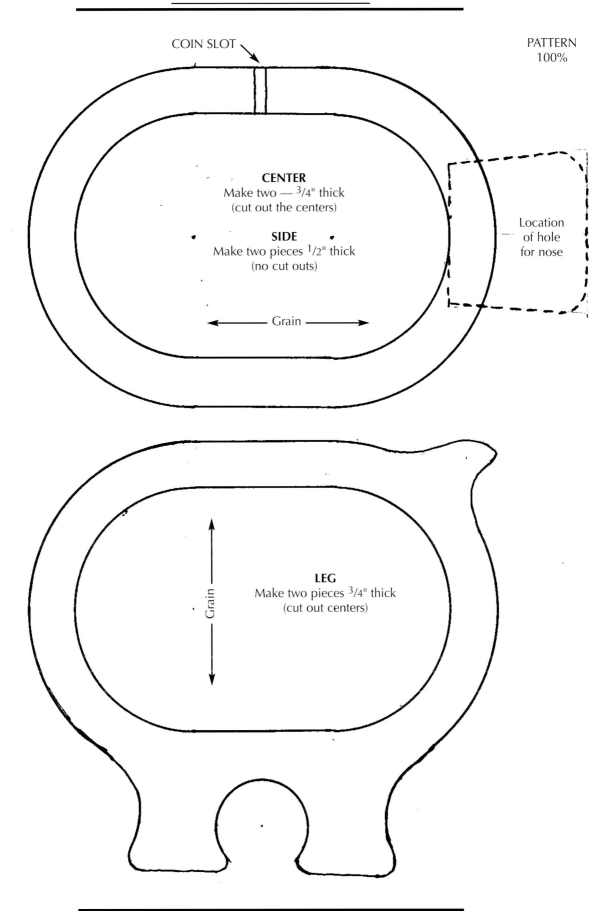

COIN SLOT

PATTERN
100%

CENTER
Make two — 3/4" thick
(cut out the centers)

SIDE
Make two pieces 1/2" thick
(no cut outs)

Grain

Location
of hole
for nose

Grain

LEG
Make two pieces 3/4" thick
(cut out centers)

Puppy Bank

Actual Height: 5¹/4"

The dog bank is made entirely of ¹/2-inch stock. Lay out and cut all the parts. Glue the three center body parts together and cut the coin slot at the top of the head. Glue the two side/leg pieces to the center assembly.

Drill the holes for the eyes. Glue a short piece of dowel, pained black, for the eye. Drill a 1¹/2 inch hole under one of the ears. Glue a plug to the back of this ear. Glue the other ear into place.

Shape as desired and apply the finish.

Puppy Bank—Pattern

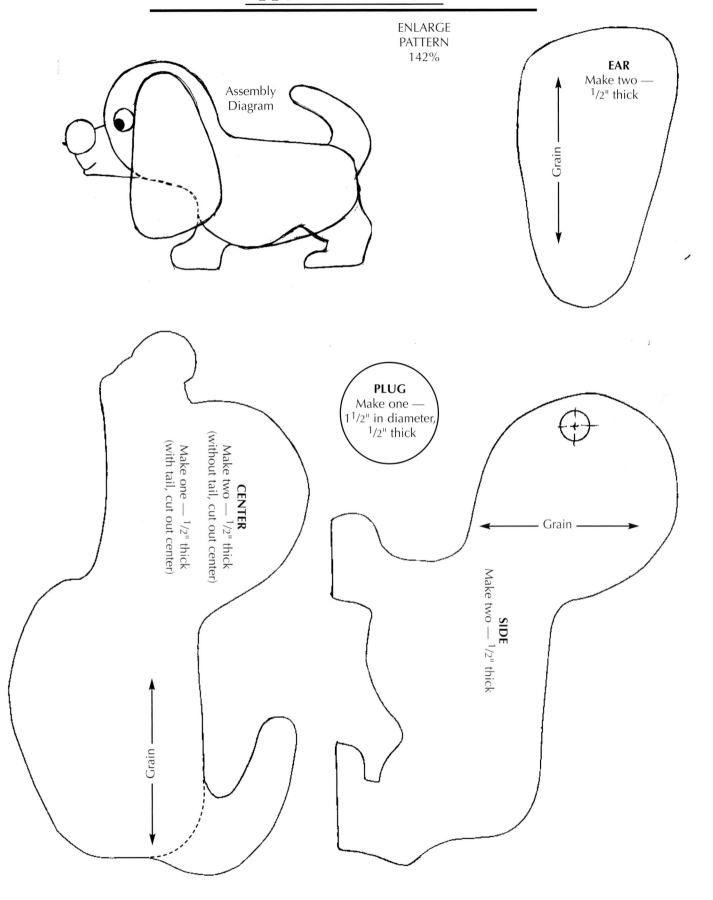

ENLARGE
PATTERN
142%

Assembly
Diagram

EAR
Make two —
1/2" thick

Grain

CENTER
Make two — 1/2" thick
(without tail, cut out center)

Make one — 1/2" thick
(with tail, cut out center)

Grain

PLUG
Make one —
1 1/2" in diameter,
1/2" thick

Grain

SIDE
Make two — 1/2" thick

River Bank

Actual Height: 5¹/₂"

This bank uses the same rectangular body structure as several other banks in this book. See page 80 for the pattern.

Make the face or front of the rectangular box from a light-colored wood; the moon and mountain should be darker pieces. Cut and sand the two mountain pieces then glue them to the front of the bank. The space between these pieces forms the river. You can color in the river with paint, if you like.

Drill a 1¹/₂-inch-diameter hole in the sky for coin removal and to receive the moon plug. The plug is made of ³/₄-inch-thick wood and stands out approximately ¹/₄ inch from the surface.

Sand all edges and apply finish as desired.

River Bank—Pattern

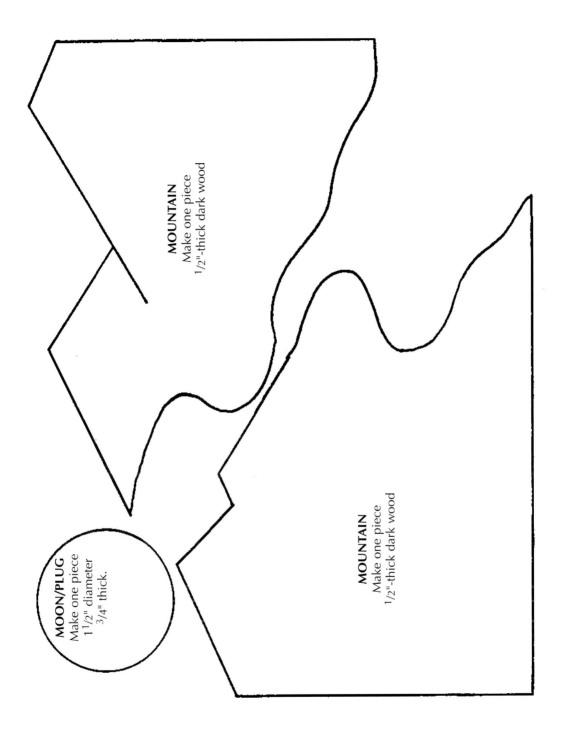

MOUNTAIN
Make one piece
1/2"-thick dark wood

MOUNTAIN
Make one piece
1/2"-thick dark wood

MOON/PLUG
Make one piece
1 1/2" diameter
3/4" thick.

Rooster Bank

Actual Height: 7¹/4"

This is an easy bank to make. All the wood should be ¹/2-inch thick. The center pieces—the tail, comb and beak—should be made from dark wood (mahogany or cherry). The rest can be light wood (pine or yellow poplar).

Begin by transferring the patterns to the wood. The leg pieces require the grain to run vertically for strength. Cut out all the pieces, including the center of the three middle pieces. Sand all the edges before assembly. Glue and clamp the center and leg pieces together. When dry, cut the coin slot straight across these parts just above the tail. This will make a slot ¹/8-inch wide and 1¹/2 inches long.

Drill a ¹/4-inch-wide hole through the head for the eyes. Drive a ¹/4-inch by 2-inch dowel through this hole for the eyes, leaving ¹/4 inch extending on each side. Glue and clamp the sides to the body. Drill a 1¹/2-diameter hole on one side under the wing position. Make a 1¹/2-inch-diameter plug, ¹/2-inch thick. File or sand a four-inch taper on the edge of the plug to make a tight fit in the body hole. Glue the plug to the back of the wing. Glue the wing to the other side.

Sand the entire bank to remove all saw marks, file marks and pencil marks. Apply the finish.

Rooter Bank—Pattern

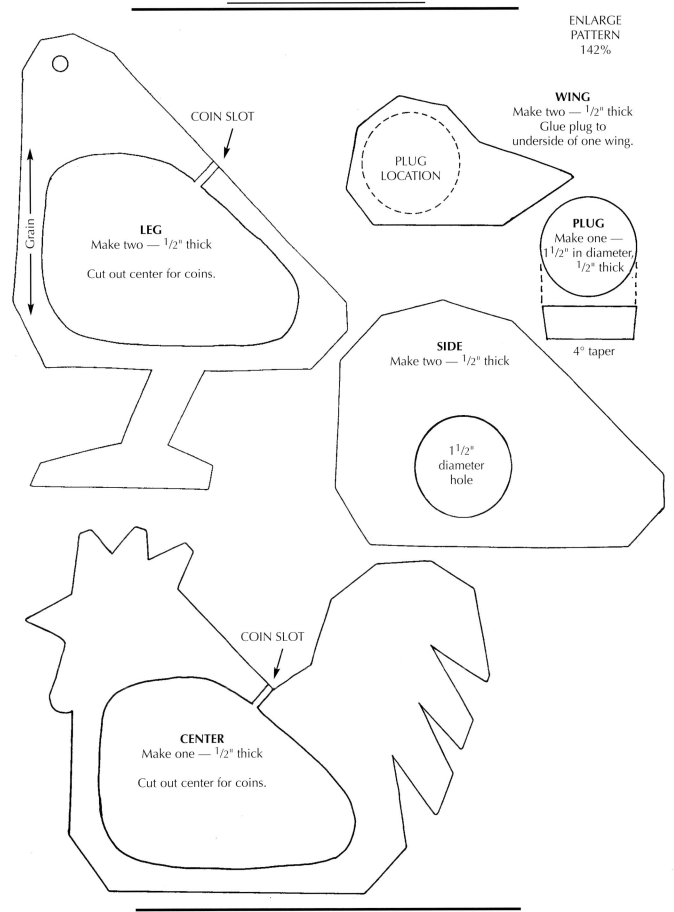

ENLARGE
PATTERN
142%

WING
Make two — 1/2" thick
Glue plug to
underside of one wing.

PLUG
LOCATION

COIN SLOT

LEG
Make two — 1/2" thick

Cut out center for coins.

Grain

PLUG
Make one —
1 1/2" in diameter,
1/2" thick

4° taper

SIDE
Make two — 1/2" thick

1 1/2"
diameter
hole

COIN SLOT

CENTER
Make one — 1/2" thick

Cut out center for coins.

Sheep Bank

Actual Height: 7³/4"

The Sheep Bank reminded me of Psalm 23, one of the most quoted Bible verses.

Lay out the body parts on ³/4-inch-thick stock. Cut the parts out. Cut out the center of all the body parts to make room for the coins. Glue two of the body pieces together and, when dry, cut the coin slot in the top. Glue all of the body parts together.

Lay out the leg parts on ³/4-inch-thick stock. Cut the parts out. Align the leg pieces and glue them to the body assembly. Drill a 1¹/2-inch hole in the front for coin removal and to fasten the head to the body.

Lay out the head parts on ¹/2-inch-thick stock. Glue the head pieces together and sand the pieces to shape. Drill the holes for the eyes. Glue a 1¹/2-inch tapered plug to the back of the head. Lay out the tail part on ¹/2-inch-thick stock and glue it to the back of the bank.

Sand until smooth and apply finish as desired.

Sheep Bank—Pattern

ENLARGE
PATTERN
111%

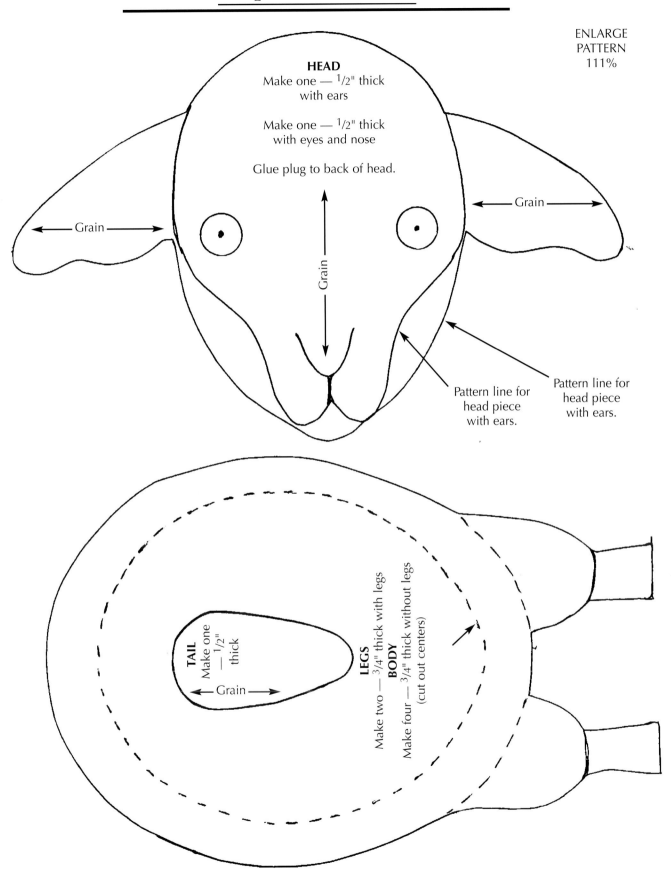

HEAD
Make one — 1/2" thick
with ears

Make one — 1/2" thick
with eyes and nose

Glue plug to back of head.

Grain

Grain

Grain

Pattern line for
head piece
with ears.

Pattern line for
head piece
with ears.

TAIL
Make one
— 1/2"
thick

Grain

LEGS
Make two — 3/4" thick with legs

BODY
Make four — 3/4" thick without legs
(cut out centers)

Smiley Face Bank

Actual Height: 6³/4"

The smile bank is very easy to make. Every one needs a smile, right? If you see some one without a smile give them one of these banks.

Lay out the parts on your stock. The two centerpieces are ³/4-inch think. Allow for a ³/4-inch flat spot at the bottom of these two pieces to receive the base piece. Cut out the center for the coin area. Glue the two pieces together. When the glue is dry cut the coin slot.

Cut out a front and back. The back is made from ¹/2-inch stock. The front is made from thin stock, such as ¹/8-inch Masonite or ¹/8-inch plywood. The Masonite makes a nice contrast in color for the smile. Glue the front and the back to the center assembly.

Cut out one more circle for the smile face from ¹/2-inch stock. Cut out the mouth and eyes. I used a router to give the edges of these cuts a nice smooth finish. Glue this to the front of the box assembly. Drill a 1¹/2-inch hole through the bottom centered between the front and back. Cut a ³/4 inch x 1¹/2 inch x 6 inch piece to fit very tightly between the front and back for the base.

Sand the ends of the base round. Finish as desired.

Smiley Face Bank—Pattern

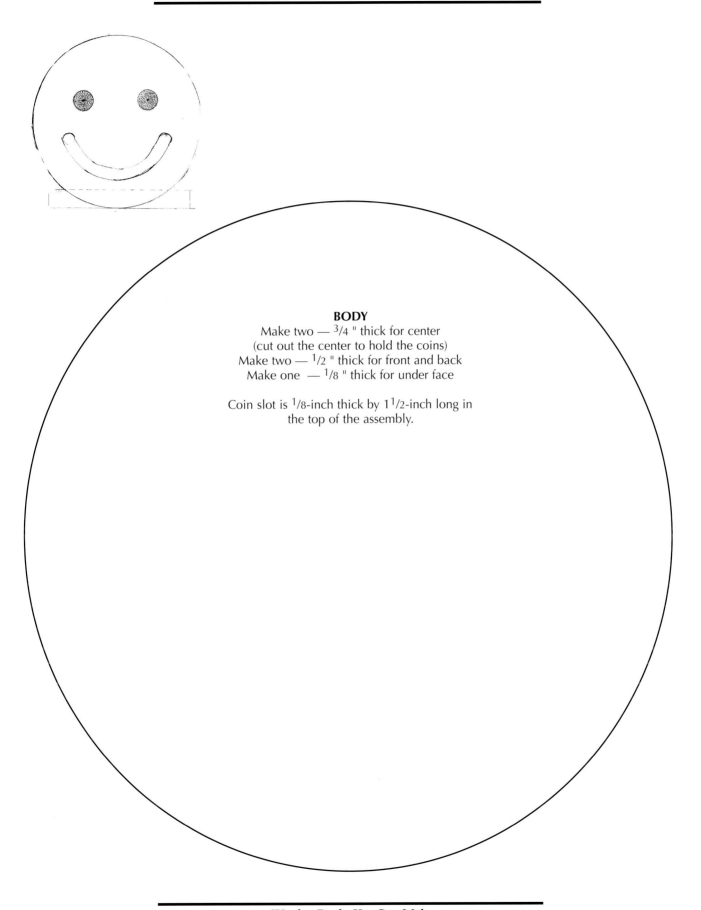

BODY
Make two — $3/4$ " thick for center
(cut out the center to hold the coins)
Make two — $1/2$ " thick for front and back
Make one — $1/8$ " thick for under face

Coin slot is $1/8$-inch thick by $1^1/2$-inch long in
the top of the assembly.

Turtle Bank

Actual Height: 3^1/$_2$"

I am a substitute teacher since my retirement. I had a long term sub position and the teacher's wife was very helpful in running the class. She loves turtles, so this is for Jeanie.

The Turtle Bank is made up of seven layers of ^{1}/$_2$-inch-thick wood. Lay out Part A on your stock and cut it out at a 45-degree angle. Trace the outer edge of Part A onto the stock for Part B. Cut out Part B at a 45-degree angle. Trace the outer edge of Part B onto the stock to get Part C. Cut Part C out at a 30-degree angle. Trace the outer edge of Part C onto the stock to make Part D. Cut Part D out at a 15-degree angle. Trace the outer edge of Part D onto the stock to get Part E Cut Part E out at a 90-degree angle.

Trace the outer edge of Part E onto the stock to get part F. Cut Part F out at a 90-degree angle. Trace Part F onto the stock to get Part G . Part G is the base and has the feet attached. Cut part G out at a 45-degree angle, but this cut the angle the opposite way to undercut the base.

Glue the bottom three pieces together and cut the ^{1}/$_2$"-thick slot for the turtle's head. Cut the turtle's head and check the fit. Make this a very tight fight. Glue the rest of the parts together to make the body of the turtle. This will give you a round smooth turtle that will need very little sanding.

Sand and finished as desired.

Turtle Bank—Pattern

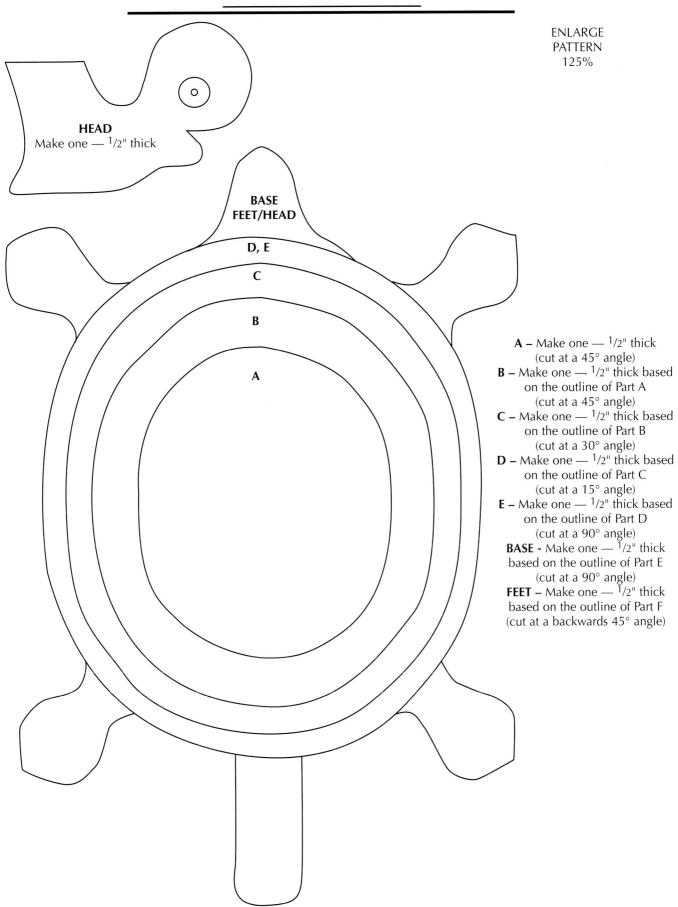

ENLARGE
PATTERN
125%

HEAD
Make one — $^1/2$" thick

**BASE
FEET/HEAD**

D, E

C

B

A

A – Make one — $^1/2$" thick
(cut at a 45° angle)
B – Make one — $^1/2$" thick based
on the outline of Part A
(cut at a 45° angle)
C – Make one — $^1/2$" thick based
on the outline of Part B
(cut at a 30° angle)
D – Make one — $^1/2$" thick based
on the outline of Part C
(cut at a 15° angle)
E – Make one — $^1/2$" thick based
on the outline of Part D
(cut at a 90° angle)
BASE - Make one — $^1/2$" thick
based on the outline of Part E
(cut at a 90° angle)
FEET – Make one — $^1/2$" thick
based on the outline of Part F
(cut at a backwards 45° angle)

Whale Bank

Actual Height: 3^1/$_2$" (not including the spout)

Lay out all the parts on ^{3}/$_4$-inch-thick wood. Note the grain direction on Parts A and B. Cut the parts out to shape. Be careful to make a clean, thin cut through Part A to cut the tail off. These parts must fit back together so the tail tilts correctly for access to the money. With all the parts cut out, glue the front half of Part A between the two Part Bs. With a damp rag, remove any glue that squeezes out where the tail will be inserted.

When the glue has set, fit the tail piece into the slot. Be sure the tail is in the correct position; then carefully drill a ^{1}/$_4$-inch-wide hole through all three pieces. Tap a ^{1}/$_4$-inch by 2^1/$_4$-inch dowel into the hole with a hammer. When the dowel is about halfway in, try to move the tail down. If the tail binds, remove the dowel and file or sand the parts where they touch. When the parts move freely, tap the dowel all the way in until it is flush with the surface. Glue Parts C to the sides of Parts B. Cut the mouth slot by sawing across all five pieces. Starting behind the eyes, sand the sides at an angle into the tail. Drill the eyes ^{1}/$_8$-inch deep with a ^{1}/$_2$-inch spade bit. File and sand the edges round and smooth.

The whale can be made with a spout if desired. Cut the spout out of ^{3}/$_4$-inch wood, file the edges round and taper the end to ^{5}/$_{16}$ round. Stain the spout blue. Drill a ^{5}/$_{16}$-inch hole in the top of the whale and insert the spout. Finish the whale as desired.

Whale Bank—Pattern

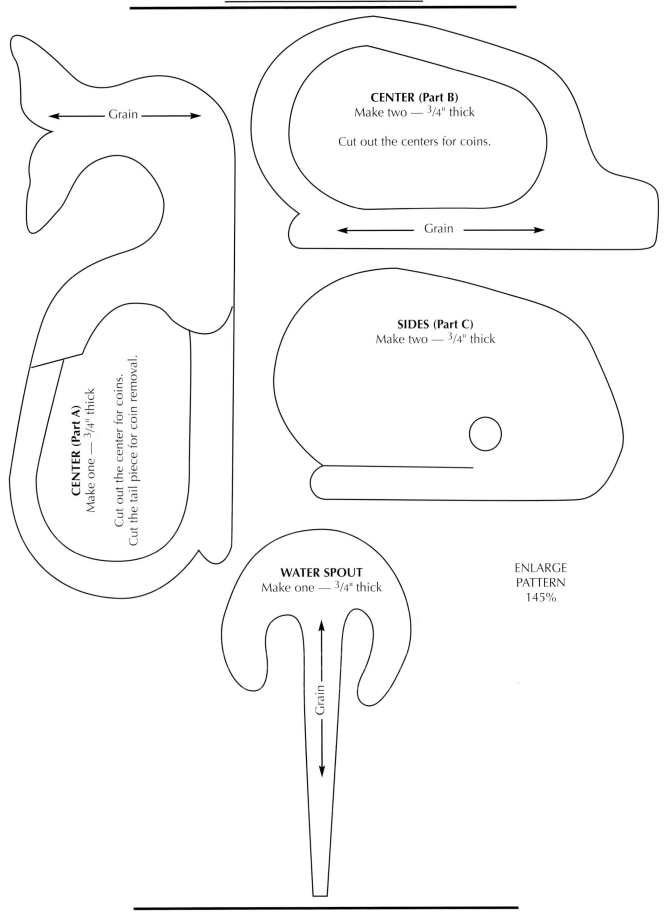

Grain

CENTER (Part B)
Make two — 3/4" thick

Cut out the centers for coins.

Grain

SIDES (Part C)
Make two — 3/4" thick

CENTER (Part A)
Make one — 3/4" thick

Cut out the center for coins.
Cut the tail piece for coin removal.

WATER SPOUT
Make one — 3/4" thick

Grain

ENLARGE
PATTERN
145%

Train Bank

Actual Height: 5³/4"

Well my editor said she wanted a train bank. Good idea. How could I refuse? Of course, it is the most complicated bank in the book. However if you take your time and read all the directions I think you will be rewarded for your effort.

Start with the front part of the engine. Make the smoke stack first (Part A). This is made with a compound cutting procedure. If you are using ³/4-inch wood you will have to glue two pieces, each measuring ³/4-inch by 1¹/2-inch by 3-inch, together to make a 1¹/2-inch by 1¹/2-inch by 3-inch piece. Fasten the pattern onto the two sides, making sure that the corner is tight against the edge of your stock. Cut one side of the smoke stack out and tape the pieces back on. Turn the piece so the uncut side is up and cut out this side. You will now have a three dimensional smoke stack.

Lay out the six round body parts on your wood (Parts B and Parts C). Cut them out in the following order. The front piece (Part C) has no hole in it. the second piece (Part C) has the top cut out to receive the smokestack. (Carefully lay the smokestack on the surface at the top and draw a like on each side with a sharp pencil. Cut through as shown on the pattern. If you leave the line showing you will get a nice tight fit, as the piece will expand just enough to force the smokestack in.) Next cut the third and forth pieces (Part C). (Cut up from the bottom removing the coin space in the middle. This cut will not show when the bank is assembled.) The fifth and sixth parts (Parts B) are larger in diameter. Cut them out as per the pattern; then re-cut the fifth piece at an 18-degree angle. This will make a nice taper from the small parts to the larger one. Remove the centers to hold the coins. Sand all these parts; then carefully glue and clamp them together.

The back of the engine is next. Lay out the parts on the wood (Parts D and Part E), paying close attention to the grain direction. Cut the parts out; then glue and clamp them together. When dry, glue and clamp the engine to the front assembly. Cut and glue some small pieces of thin stock, such as Masonite, to the inside of the cabin to cover the windows and to keep the coins from falling out.

Cut the roof (Part F). Add a coin slot, $1/8$-inch wide by $1^1/2$-inch long, centered over the cabin cavity. Cut a $3/4$ inch by 3-inch by 12 inch strip of wood to fit very snugly inside the sides of the cabin. This will form the bottom of the engine (Part G). Lay out and cut the compound cuts on the front of this piece to made the cowcatcher. About six inches back from the front, cut this piece in two at a 45-degree angle. Glue and clamp the front part to the bottom of the front engine assembly.

Cut out the six wheels (Part H and Part I). This can be done on the scroll saw or, if you have a drill press, you can use a hole saw. Cut and glue the two spacers (Part J) to the front of the engine bottom, to make the front wheels line up with the rear wheels. Lay out and drill the holes for the axles. The $5/32$-inch holes give clearance for the $1/4$-inch dowel axles. Drill the holes halfway from each side to make sure they will line up all the way through. The rear axle holds the bottom in until you want to remove the money. To remove the money, take off the rear wheel and axle and pull the bottom back and down.

Sand until smooth and apply the finish of your choice.

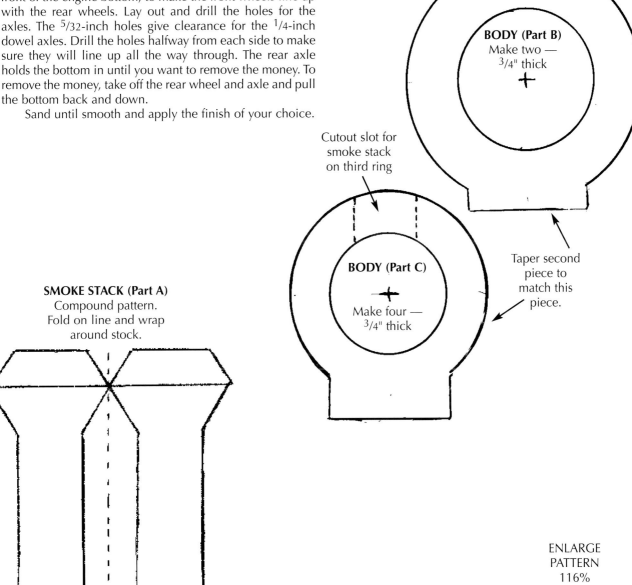

Cutout slot for smoke stack on third ring

BODY (Part B)
Make two —
$3/4$" thick

Taper second piece to match this piece.

BODY (Part C)

Make four —
$3/4$" thick

SMOKE STACK (Part A)
Compound pattern.
Fold on line and wrap
around stock.

ENLARGE
PATTERN
116%

Train Bank—Pattern

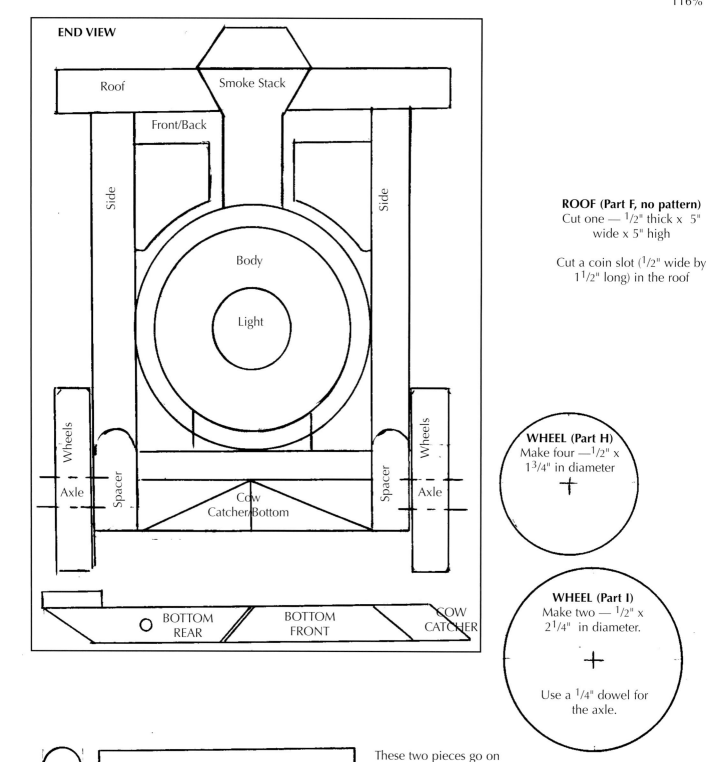

END VIEW

Roof

Smoke Stack

Front/Back

Side

Side

Body

Light

Wheels

Wheels

Axle

Spacer

Spacer

Axle

Cow
Catcher/Bottom

BOTTOM
REAR

BOTTOM
FRONT

COW
CATCHER

ROOF (Part F, no pattern)
Cut one — $1/2$" thick x 5"
wide x 5" high

Cut a coin slot ($1/2$" wide by
$1^1/2$" long) in the roof

WHEEL (Part H)
Make four — $1/2$" x
$1^3/4$" in diameter

WHEEL (Part I)
Make two — $1/2$" x
$2^1/4$" in diameter.

Use a $1/4$" dowel for
the axle.

SPACERS (Part J)
Make two —
$1/2$" x $1^1/4$" x $3^1/4$"

These two pieces go on
both sides of the front
assembly They butt up
against the front edge of the
cab to make the front
wheels line up with the
back wheels.

Wooden Banks You Can Make

Train Bank—Pattern

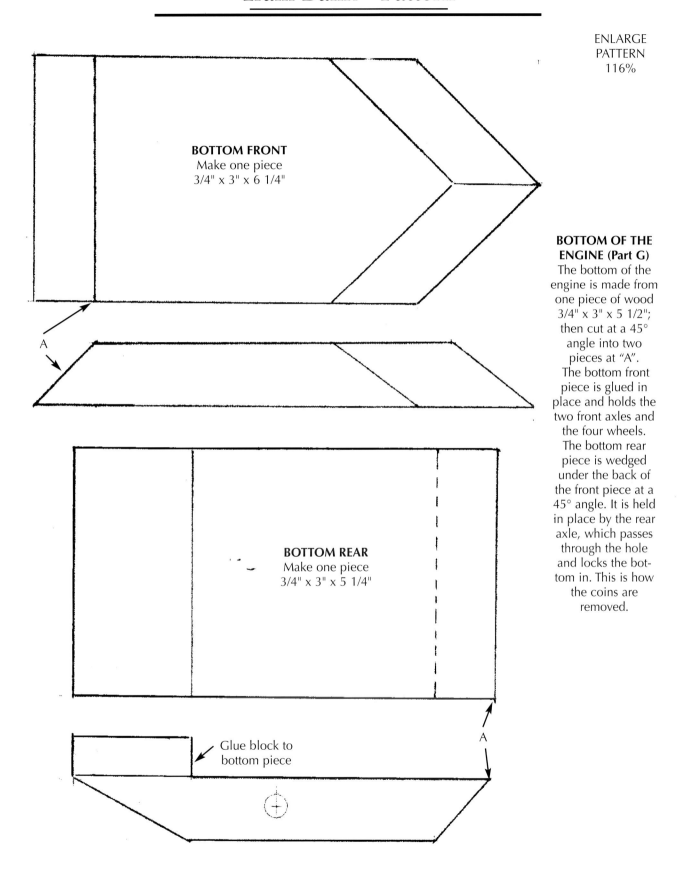

BOTTOM FRONT
Make one piece
3/4" x 3" x 6 1/4"

A

BOTTOM REAR
Make one piece
3/4" x 3" x 5 1/4"

Glue block to
bottom piece

A

ENLARGE
PATTERN
116%

**BOTTOM OF THE
ENGINE (Part G)**
The bottom of the
engine is made from
one piece of wood
3/4" x 3" x 5 1/2";
then cut at a 45°
angle into two
pieces at "A".
The bottom front
piece is glued in
place and holds the
two front axles and
the four wheels.
The bottom rear
piece is wedged
under the back of
the front piece at a
45° angle. It is held
in place by the rear
axle, which passes
through the hole
and locks the bot-
tom in. This is how
the coins are
removed.

Train Bank—Pattern

ENLARGE
PATTERN
116%

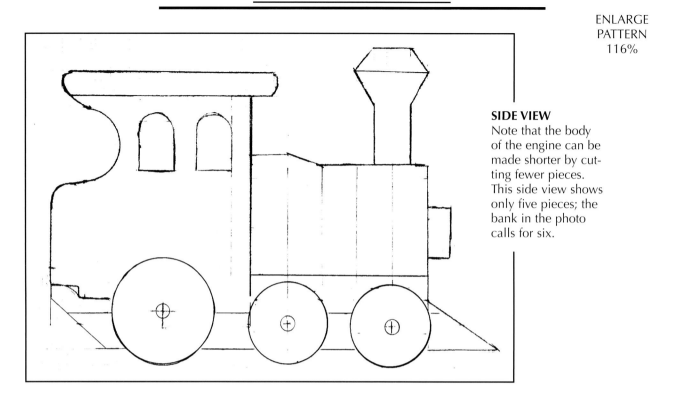

SIDE VIEW
Note that the body
of the engine can be
made shorter by cut-
ting fewer pieces.
This side view shows
only five pieces; the
bank in the photo
calls for six.

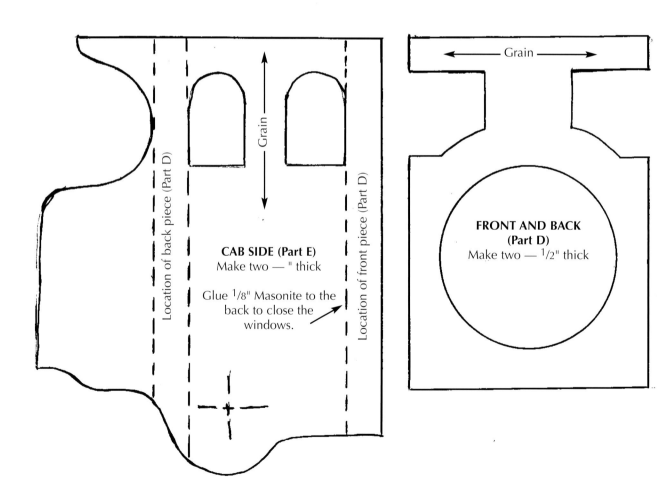

Location of back piece (Part D)

CAB SIDE (Part E)
Make two — " thick

Glue $1/8$" Masonite to the
back to close the
windows.

Location of front piece (Part D)

Grain

Grain

**FRONT AND BACK
(Part D)**
Make two — $1/2$" thick

Cow Bank

Actual Height: 7^1/$_2$"

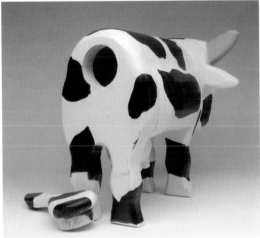

Our kitchen looks like the Cracker Barrel Restaurant. Our neighbor says my wife is the Cracker Barrel Queen. Every square inch of wall is covered by something collectable or some memento from our past. One of these items is a cut-out of a cow. My wife wanted a cow bank....

Before you begin, note that both the head and the tail are removable on this bank.

Lay out the parts on your stock and cut them out. Glue the two parts together that will have the coin slot and cut the slot through to the inside. (Note: The udder is made of two pieces, this makes it much easier to make.) Glue and clamp the body parts together, making sure to get them lined up for minimum sanding later. Glue and clamp the head parts. Drill a 1^1/$_2$-thick-inch hole into the front and back legs for the head and tail plug.

Sand all sharp edges round and smooth. Apply the finish of your choice. I think she looks best painted.

Cow Bank—Pattern

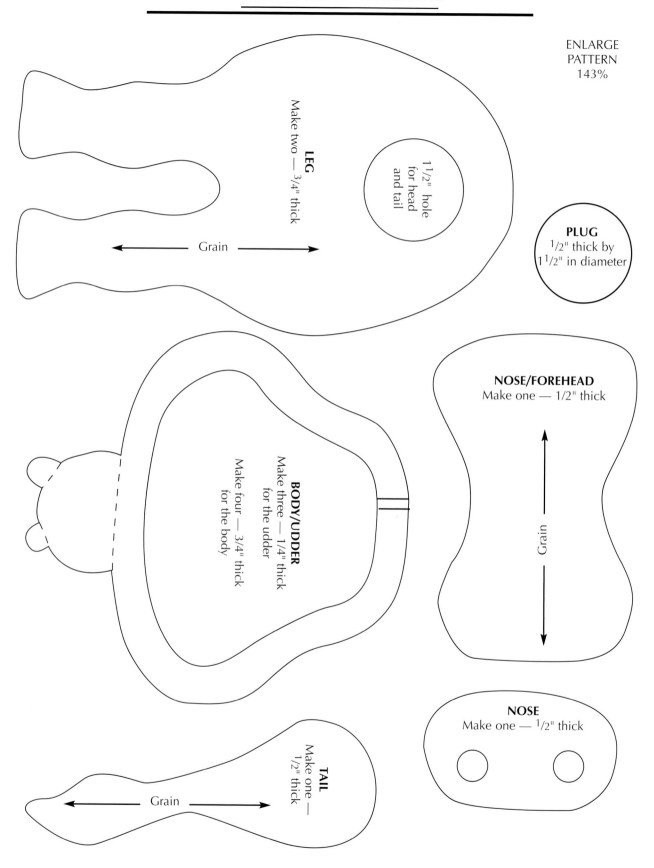

ENLARGE
PATTERN
143%

LEG
Make two — 3/4" thick

1 1/2" hole
for head
and tail

Grain

PLUG
1/2" thick by
1 1/2" in diameter

NOSE/FOREHEAD
Make one — 1/2" thick

BODY/UDDER
Make three — 1/4" thick
for the udder

Make four — 3/4" thick
for the body

Grain

TAIL
Make one —
1/2" thick

Grain

NOSE
Make one — 1/2" thick

Cow Bank—Pattern

ENLARGE
PATTERN
143%

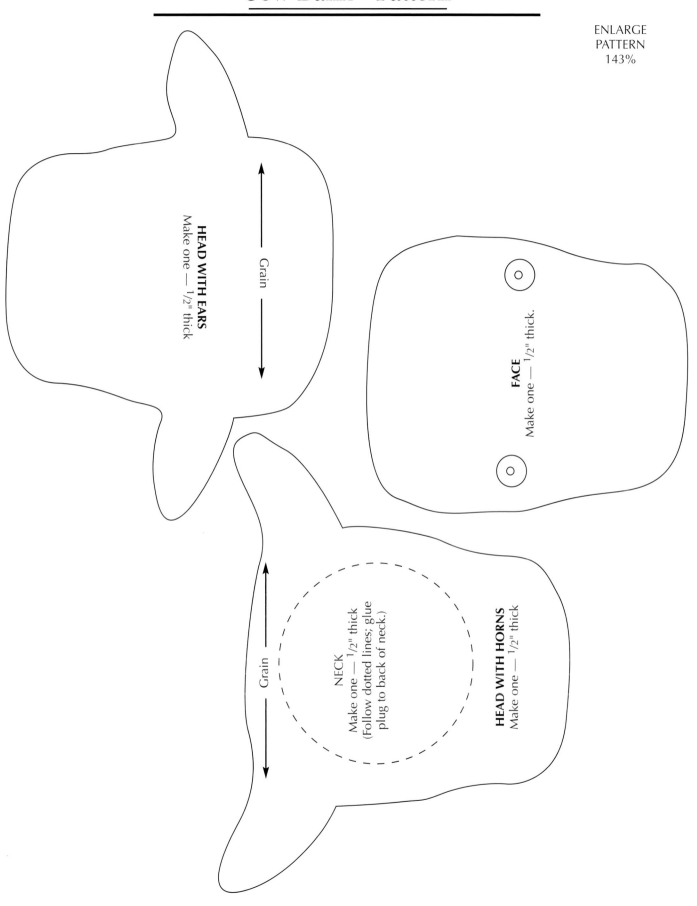

HEAD WITH EARS
Make one — $1/2$" thick

Grain

FACE
Make one — $1/2$" thick.

NECK
Make one — $1/2$" thick
(Follow dotted lines; glue
plug to back of neck.)

Grain

HEAD WITH HORNS
Make one — $1/2$" thick

Duck Bank

Actual Height: 6¹/₂"

Lay out the parts on the stock. The center piece is ³/₄-inch thick. The cheek pieces are ³/₈-inch thick. (These pieces can be cut out of ³/₄"-inch thick stock and then re-sawn on the band saw. The resulting parts are a skinny ³/₈-inch thick.)

Cut out the center piece and the cheek pieces. Cut the coin slot and remove the area that holds the coins. Glue these three pieces together; then glue the sides to this assembly.

Drill the eye holes about ¹/₄-inch deep. Drill the 1¹/₂-inch hole for the coin removal under one of the wing positions. Glue the other wing into position on the other side.

Sand and shape until smooth and nicely rounded. Apply the finish of your choice.

Duck Bank—Pattern

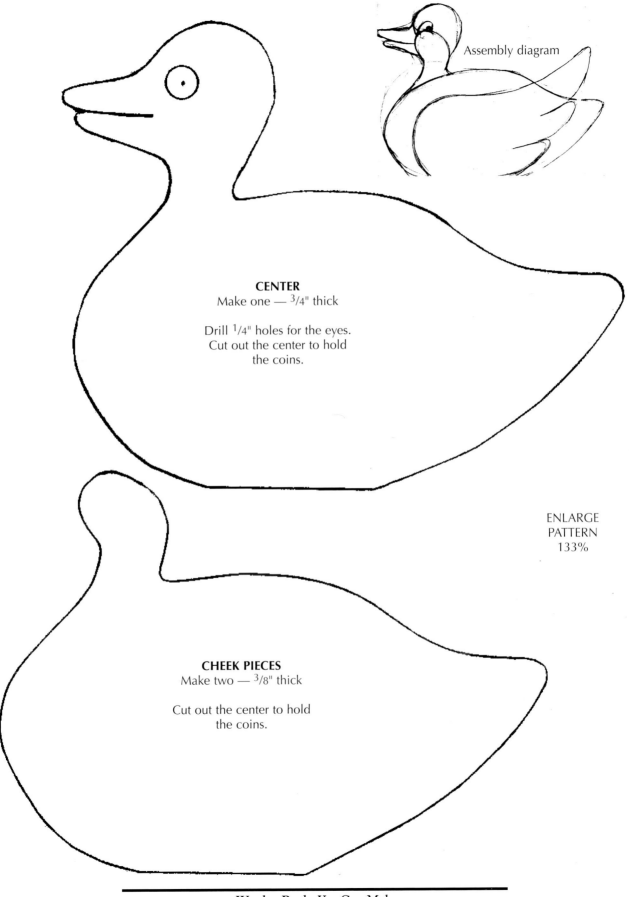

Assembly diagram

CENTER
Make one — 3/4" thick

Drill 1/4" holes for the eyes.
Cut out the center to hold
the coins.

ENLARGE
PATTERN
133%

CHEEK PIECES
Make two — 3/8" thick

Cut out the center to hold
the coins.

Duck Bank—Pattern

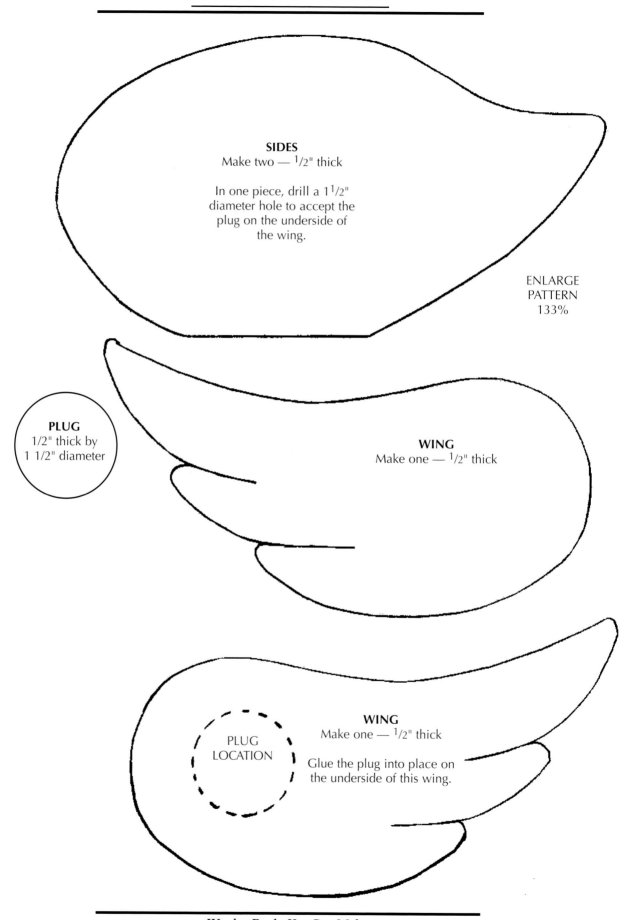

SIDES
Make two — $^1/_2$" thick

In one piece, drill a $1^1/_2$" diameter hole to accept the plug on the underside of the wing.

ENLARGE PATTERN 133%

PLUG
1/2" thick by 1 1/2" diameter

WING
Make one — $^1/_2$" thick

WING
Make one — $^1/_2$" thick

Glue the plug into place on the underside of this wing.

PLUG LOCATION

Fox Bank

Actual Height: 10³/4"

Lay out the parts on ³/4-inch-thick wood and cut them to shape. The body (ring) parts are 3¹/2-inch-diameter circles with a 2¹/2-inch-diameter holes in the middle. There will be less chance of breakage if the holes are cut first. Glue two rings together and cut a ¹/8-inch-wide by 1¹/2-inch-long coin slot through the top into the center. Glue a ring on each side of these two rings.

Glue the two face pieces together. Drill the eyes ¹/8-inch-deep using a ¹/2-inch spade bit. The head must be well-rounded. Use a rasp, file and sandpaper to remove all sharpness. Drill a 1¹/2-inch-diameter hole through the top of the piece forming the front legs. Taper a 1¹/2-inch-diameter plug to fit tightly into this hole. Glue the plug to the neck piece and the neck to the back of the head.

The tail can be glued to the back leg piece or held with a ³/4-inch dowel , if you wish to the tail to move. Glue the leg pieces to the body.

File and sand all edges smooth and round. Finish as desired.

Fox Bank—Pattern

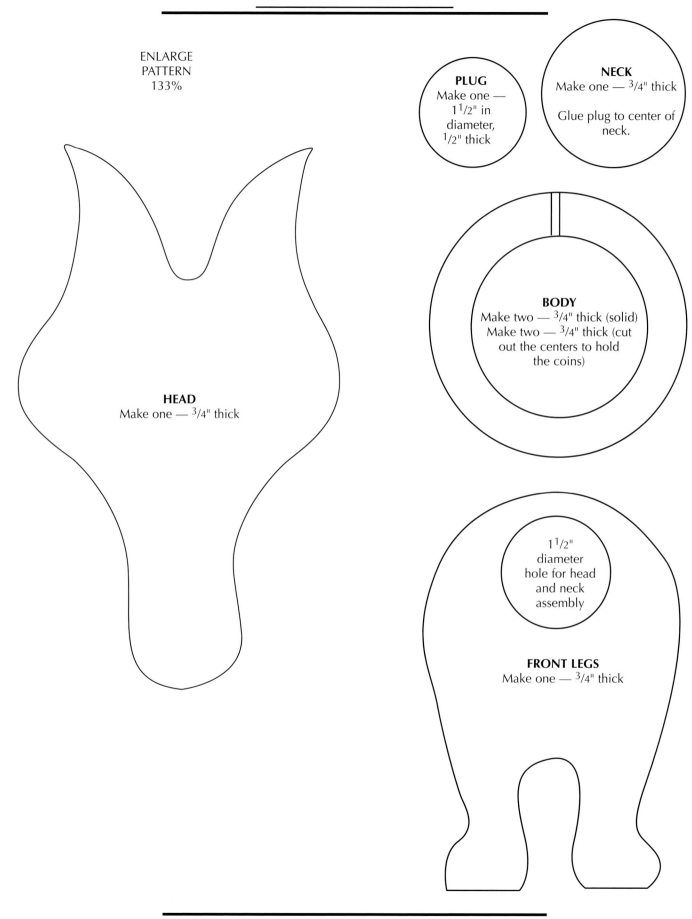

ENLARGE
PATTERN
133%

PLUG
Make one —
1 1/2" in
diameter,
1/2" thick

NECK
Make one — 3/4" thick

Glue plug to center of
neck.

HEAD
Make one — 3/4" thick

BODY
Make two — 3/4" thick (solid)
Make two — 3/4" thick (cut
out the centers to hold
the coins)

1 1/2"
diameter
hole for head
and neck
assembly

FRONT LEGS
Make one — 3/4" thick

Fox Bank—Pattern

ENLARGE
PATTERN
133%

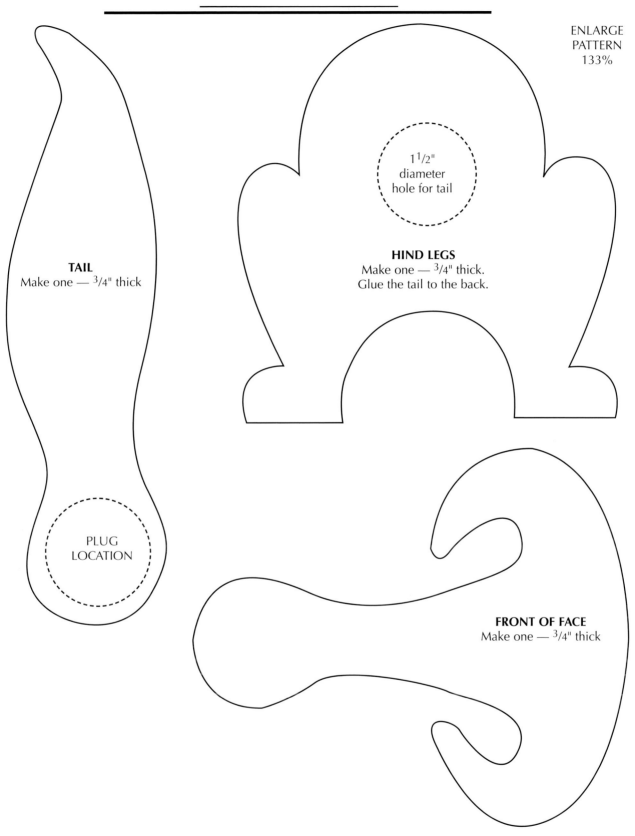

TAIL
Make one — 3/4" thick

PLUG
LOCATION

1 1/2"
diameter
hole for tail

HIND LEGS
Make one — 3/4" thick.
Glue the tail to the back.

FRONT OF FACE
Make one — 3/4" thick

Gator Bank

Actual Height: 8"

This bank has quite a story behind it. Through shoulder surgery, I met Dr. Peter Indelicato, the team physician for the University of Florida's football team. He has many trophies from famous athletes in his office showcase. I always teased him about how I could get my name in the case. Well, I made "Albert;" and now Albert is in the case with his arm in a sling next to a very famous person. This bank is dedicated to you Dr. Pete.

The Gator Bank can be made either with the tail upright or straight out the back. Simply rotate the pattern. The straight tail makes the bank easier to sand and finish.

You will need some 1/8-inch stock—Masonite works well—and some 1/2-inch stock. Any softwood such as pine or plywood will do because this bank looks best painted.

Lay out Part A on the 1/8-inch stock and cut it out. Do not cut the mouth out at this time. Lay out and cut two of Part B from 1/2-inch stock. Glue and clamp Part A between the two Part Bs. Cut out the mouth on this assembly.

Lay out two of Part C on 1/8-inch stock and cut them out. Lay out two of Part D on 1/2-inch stock and cut them out. Glue and clamp these four pieces to the center assembly. You now have a Gator body that has teeth and bumps on its back and tail.

Smooth out this assembly, both outside and the inside coin chamber. Lay out and cut out two Part E (sides) from 1/2-inch stock. Round the outside corners of these parts and glue them to the sides of the body.

Lay out and cut out the four legs from 1/2-inch stock. Drill 1 1/2-inch holes for coin removal under where the leg will go. Glue a tapered plug to the back of the leg for access to the coin chamber. (You can make all the legs and arms movable, if desired, by drilling a hole for a tapered plug under each leg and arm.)

For his front teeth, drill a hole near the front of the lower jaw at an angle on each side so they will come up over the upper jaw. Sharpen a dowel in a pencil sharpener and glue it into the hole drilled on each side.

Paint the teeth and eyes black. Paint the eye socket white. Paint the body dark green. The Gator Bank that I made for Dr. Pete has an orange sweater with a blue "F" on the front.

Gator Bank—Pattern

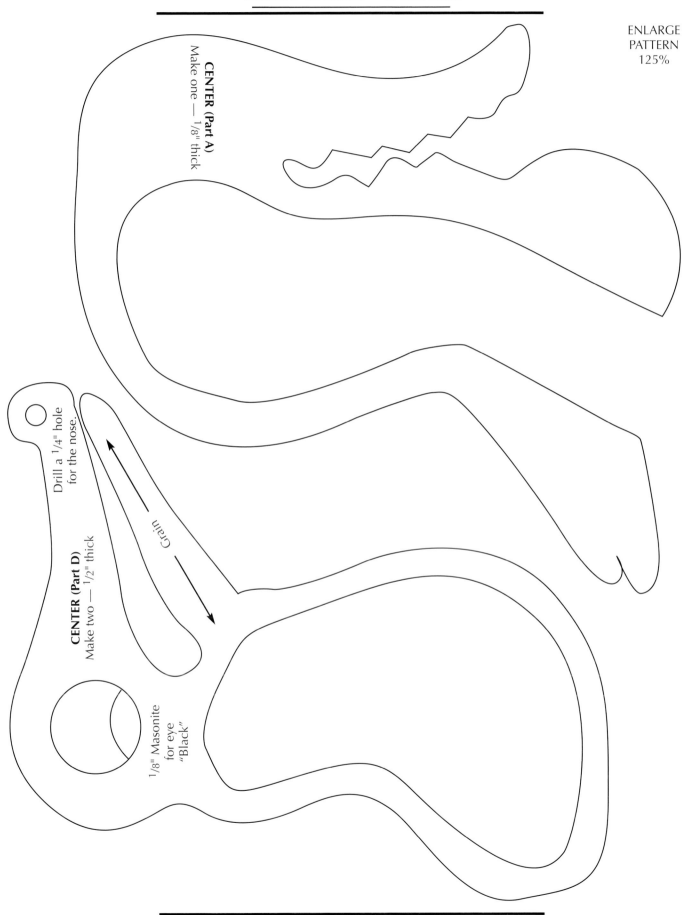

ENLARGE
PATTERN
125%

CENTER (Part A)
Make one — 1/8" thick

Drill a 1/4" hole
for the nose.

Grain

CENTER (Part D)
Make two — 1/2" thick

1/8" Masonite
for eye
"Black"

Gator Bank—Pattern

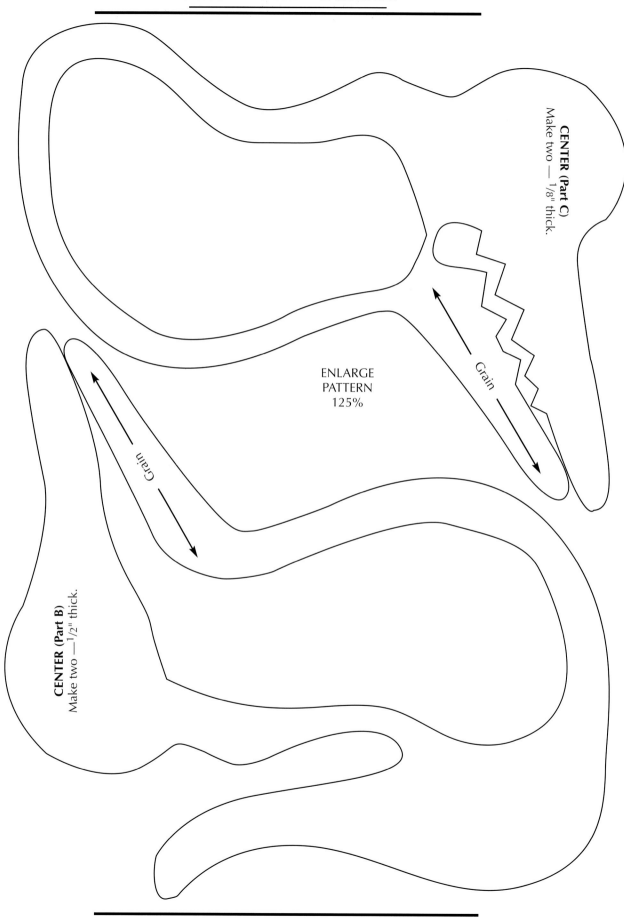

CENTER (Part C)
Make two — 1/8" thick.

Grain

ENLARGE
PATTERN
125%

Grain

CENTER (Part B)
Make two — 1/2" thick.

Gator Bank—Pattern

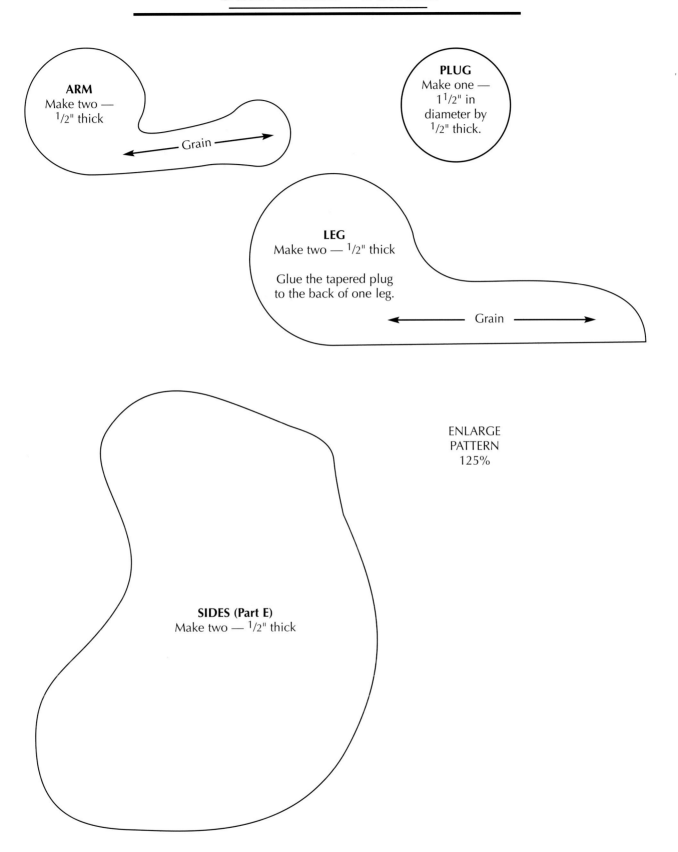

ARM
Make two —
$1/2$" thick

Grain

PLUG
Make one —
$1^{1}/2$" in
diameter by
$1/2$" thick.

LEG
Make two — $1/2$" thick

Glue the tapered plug
to the back of one leg.

Grain

ENLARGE
PATTERN
125%

SIDES (Part E)
Make two — $1/2$" thick

Moose Bank

Actual Height: 8¹/2"

Lay out the pattern for the moose on ¹/2-inch-thick wood. Make the nose and antlers of dark wood, such as mahogany. The rest of the moose can be made from a lighter colored wood, such as pine. Drill or saw out the middle of each piece before sawing the outline to shape; this will reduce the chance of breaking the pieces. When the pieces are cut to shape, glue the head piece together. Align it carefully to avoid filing and sanding later. The antlers and corresponding head pieces are located next to the back. The antlers should be the same thickness or made from the same piece of wood as the head piece below them. This will make a tight fit for the removable antlers. When gluing the head pieces, be careful to remove all the excess glue.

Drill or cut out the center of two of the nose pieces; then cut the outside to shape. Glue the three nose pieces together offsetting each a little to create a long, drooping nose. When dry, rasp, file and sand the nose to remove all corners or sharp edges. Glue the nose into place on the head. Use a chisel to make a ¹/8-inch-deep by 1¹/2-inch-wide coin slot on the dotted lines of the antlers.

Drill holes for eyes and the nostrils. Apply finish as desired.

Moose Bank—Pattern

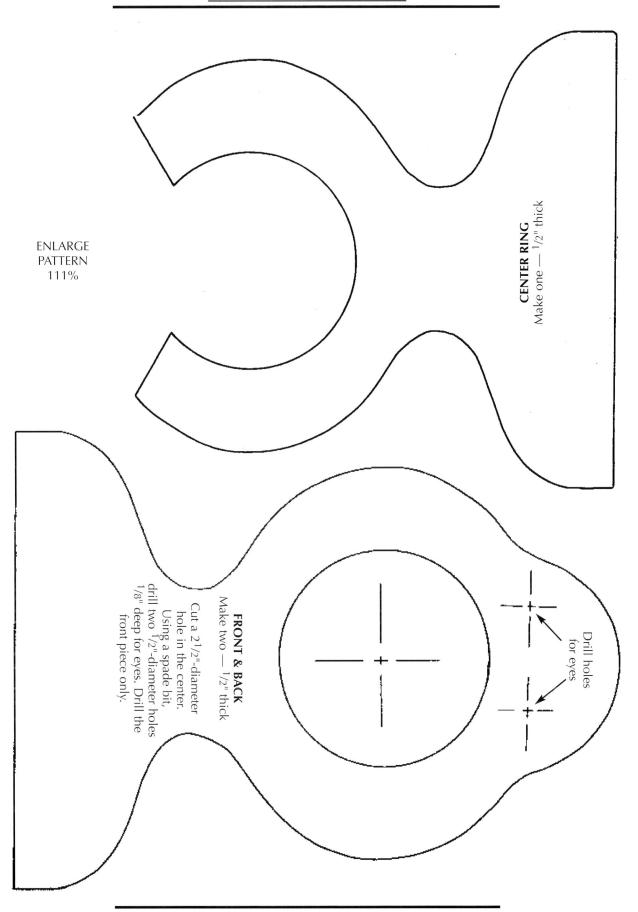

ENLARGE PATTERN 111%

CENTER RING
Make one — 1/2" thick

FRONT & BACK
Make two — 1/2" thick

Cut a 2 1/2"-diameter hole in the center. Using a spade bit, drill two 1/2"-diameter holes 1/8" deep for eyes. Drill the front piece only.

Drill holes for eyes

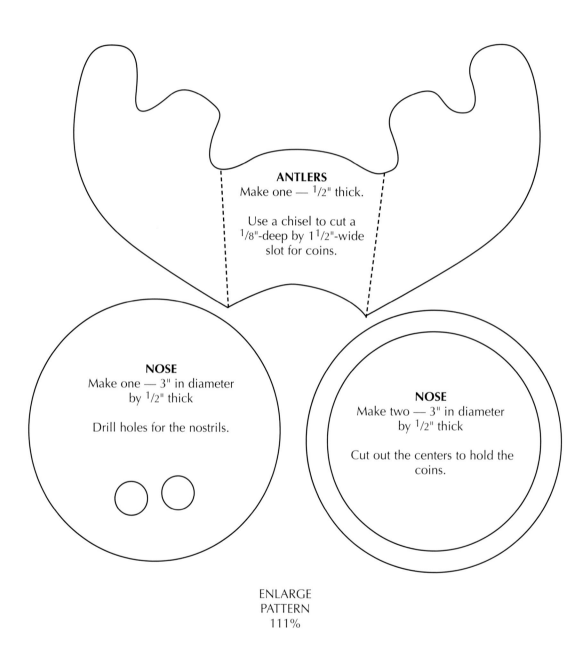

ANTLERS
Make one — 1/2" thick.

Use a chisel to cut a
1/8"-deep by 1 1/2"-wide
slot for coins.

NOSE
Make one — 3" in diameter
by 1/2" thick

Drill holes for the nostrils.

NOSE
Make two — 3" in diameter
by 1/2" thick

Cut out the centers to hold the
coins.

ENLARGE
PATTERN
111%

Teapot Bank

Actual Height: 5"

My mother had a small teapot similar to this on her sink. She would use it to keep her rings safe while she was doing the dishes.

The Tea Pot Bank is an easy bank to make. The important thing to remember is to be accurate in your cutting. The closer you follow the lines, the less sanding you will have to do. Cut the centerpiece, with the handle and spout, first. Make your entry to the inside through the coin slot at the top of the handle. Cut out the inside leaving about half an inch of wood to form the frame.

Cut the two $1/2$-inch-thick side pieces next. Don't forget to cut away the center where the coins will be stored. Glue and clamp these pieces, one on each side of the center piece. Carefully line up the three parts to avoid handwork later.

The two outside pieces are $3/4$-inch thick. These pieces are solid and form the outside of the bank. Once you have them cut out, turn them upside-down, tilt the table on your saw to 45 degrees, then cut around the edge. This will produce a nice chamfer around the out side of the tea pot. (If you have access to a drill and Forstner bit, you can drill out the inside of these parts to make more room for the money.) Clamp and glue these two outside pieces to the center assembly.

Drill a $1^1/2$-inch-diameter hole in the center of the top of the tea pot to the inside cavity. Cut out a $1^1/2$-inch-diameter plug from $1/2$-inch-thick scrap. Tilt the saw table about 5 degrees or use a disc sander to create a slight taper on the sides of the plug. Make several trial fits to avoid making the plug too loose. The top of the plug is a hexagon, two inches across at the flats. Slightly chamfer the top and bottom edges. Glue the plug to the center of the top.

Sand the entire bank until it is smooth. Apply the finish of your choice.

Teapot Bank—Pattern

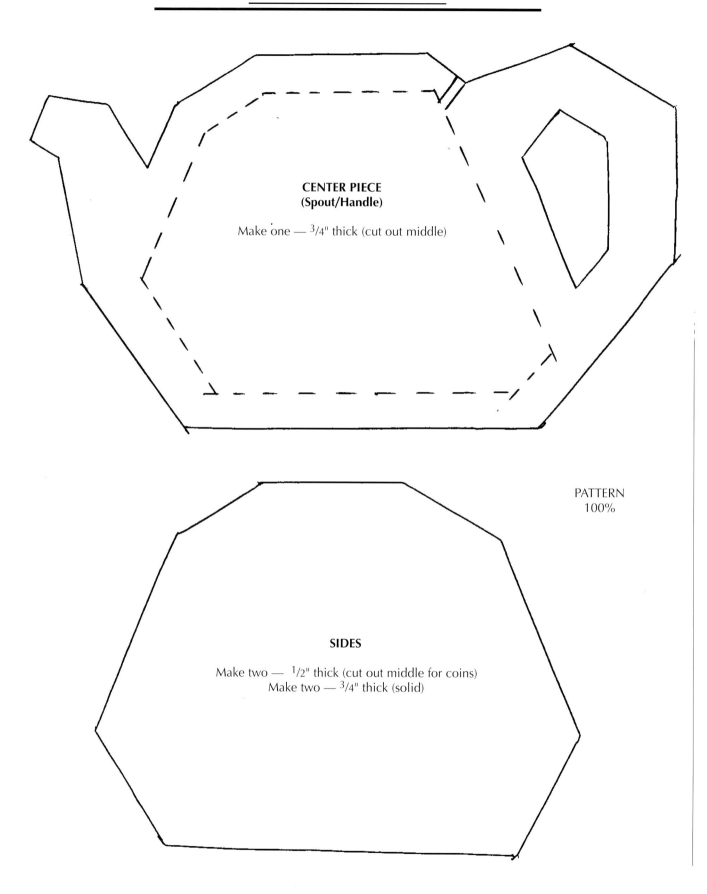

**CENTER PIECE
(Spout/Handle)**

Make one — 3/4" thick (cut out middle)

PATTERN
100%

SIDES

Make two — 1/2" thick (cut out middle for coins)
Make two — 3/4" thick (solid)

Teapot Bank—Pattern

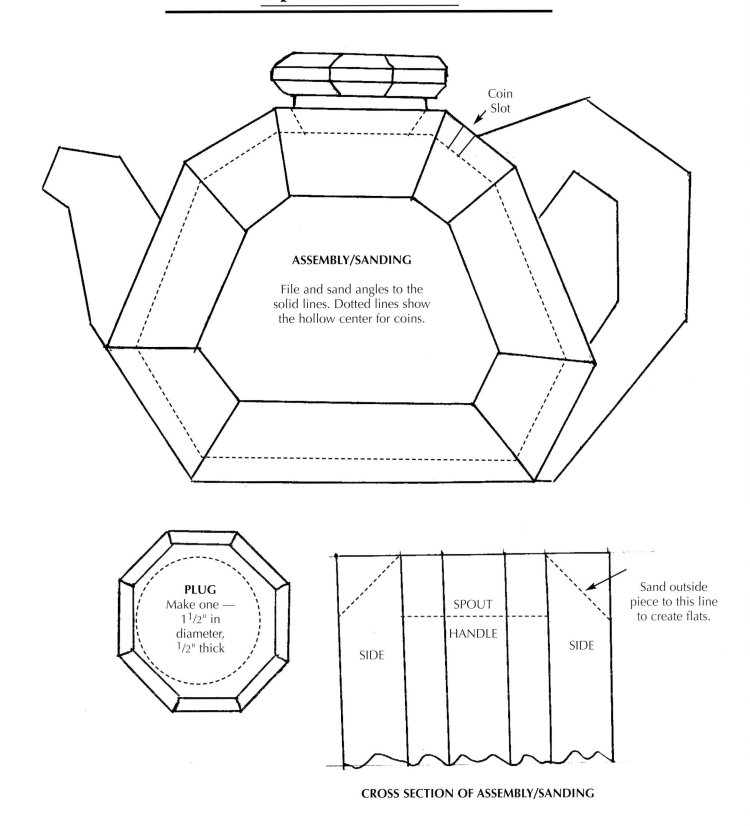

Coin
Slot

ASSEMBLY/SANDING

File and sand angles to the
solid lines. Dotted lines show
the hollow center for coins.

PLUG
Make one —
1 1/2" in
diameter,
1/2" thick

SPOUT

HANDLE

SIDE

SIDE

Sand outside
piece to this line
to create flats.

CROSS SECTION OF ASSEMBLY/SANDING

Box Pattern

(Use for all rectangular banks.)

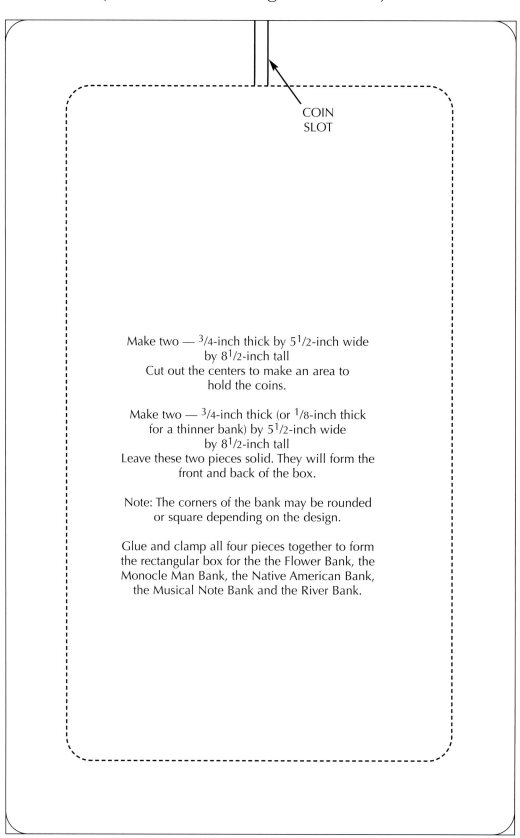

COIN
SLOT

Make two — $3/4$-inch thick by $5^1/2$-inch wide
by $8^1/2$-inch tall
Cut out the centers to make an area to
hold the coins.

Make two — $3/4$-inch thick (or $1/8$-inch thick
for a thinner bank) by $5^1/2$-inch wide
by $8^1/2$-inch tall
Leave these two pieces solid. They will form the
front and back of the box.

Note: The corners of the bank may be rounded
or square depending on the design.

Glue and clamp all four pieces together to form
the rectangular box for the the Flower Bank, the
Monocle Man Bank, the Native American Bank,
the Musical Note Bank and the River Bank.

SUBSCRIBE TODAY!

DON'T MISS ANOTHER ISSUE OF SCROLL SAW WORKSHOP

☐ **ONE YEAR** Subscription

☐ $19.95 USA
☐ $22.50 Canada - US Funds Only
☐ $27.95 Int'l - US Funds Only

☐ **TWO YEAR** Subscription

☐ $39.90 USA
☐ $45.00 Canada - US Funds Only
☐ $55.90 Int'l - US Funds Only

Please allow 4-6 weeks for delivery

Four issues per year

☐ Bill Me   ☐ Check/Money Order
☐ Visa, MC or Discover

Name on card _____

Exp. date _____ Telephone ( ) _____
cardnumber
☐☐☐☐☐☐☐☐☐☐☐☐☐☐☐☐☐

Send To:

Name: _____
Address: _____
_____
City: _____
State/Prov.: _____
Zip: _____
Telephone: _____ Country: _____

VISA MasterCard DISCOVER NOVUS   **CFBN**

SCROLL SAW TOYS AND VEHICLES
A Complete Technique and Project Pattern Manual
By Stan Graves

FREE with a two-year paid subscription

Subscription order desk 888-840-8590

SUBSCRIBE TODAY!

DON'T MISS ANOTHER ISSUE OF WOOD CARVING ILLUSTRATED

☐ **ONE YEAR** Subscription

☐ $19.95 USA
☐ $22.50 Canada - US Funds Only
☐ $27.95 Int'l - US Funds Only

☐ **TWO YEAR** Subscription

☐ $39.90 USA
☐ $45.00 Canada - US Funds Only
☐ $55.90 Int'l - US Funds Only

Please allow 4-6 weeks for delivery

Four issues per year

☐ Bill Me   ☐ Check/Money Order
☐ Visa, MC or Discover

Name on card _____

Exp. date _____ Telephone ( ) _____
cardnumber
☐☐☐☐☐☐☐☐☐☐☐☐☐☐☐☐☐

Send To:

Name: _____
Address: _____
_____
City: _____
State/Prov.: _____
Zip: _____
Telephone: _____ Country: _____

VISA MasterCard DISCOVER NOVUS   **CFBN**

How to Carve Wood - over 500+ color photos
Power Carving MANUAL
A Special Edition from your friends at Wood Carving Illustrated Magazine
BIRD CARVING Step-by-Step
207 Bits & Burs for Carvers
Carving Gun Stocks
Sign Making
Most Complete Tool Reference Available

FREE with a two-year paid subscription

Subscription order desk: 888-506-6630

FREE BOOK CATALOG

YES! *I'd like a free catalog of your woodworking titles. Please place me on your mailing list and send me a copy right away.*

Previously purchased titles:
_____
_____

I'm particularly interested in: *(circle all that apply)*   General Woodworking   Woodcarving   Scroll Sawing   Cabinetmaking   Nature Drawing

Suggestion box: I think Fox Chapel should do a book about:
_____
_____

Bonus: Give us your email address to receive free updates.

Send to:
Name: _____   Email Address: _____
Address: _____   City: _____
State/Prov.: _____
Telephone: _____ Country: _____ Zip: _____

**Visit us on the web at www.Foxchapelpublishing.com
or call us at 800-457-9112**

AFB00

1970 Broad St.
East Petersburg PA 17520   USA

Wood Carving
ILLUSTRATED

1970 Broad St.
East Petersburg PA 17520   USA

Fox
Chapel Publishing Co. Inc.

Free Catalog Offer
1970 Broad St.
East Petersburg PA 17520   USA